D0902991

# HIGH SCHOOL FOOTBALL RULES
# SIMPLIFIED & ILLUSTRATED
# 2023

**Dr. KARISSA L. NIEHOFF, Publisher**
Bob Colgate, Editor
**NFHS Publications**

To maintain the sound traditions of this sport, encourage sportsmanship and minimize the inherent risk of injury, the National Federation of State High School Associations (NFHS) writes playing rules for varsity competition among student-athletes of high school age. High school coaches, game officials and administrators who have knowledge and experience regarding this particular sport and age group volunteer their time to serve on the rules committee. Member associations of the NFHS independently make decisions regarding compliance with or modification of the playing rules for the student-athletes in their respective states.

NFHS rules are used by education-based and non-education-based organizations serving children of varying skill levels who are of high school age and younger. In order to make NFHS rules skill-level and age-level appropriate, the rules may be modified by any organization that chooses to use them. Except as may be specifically noted in the NFHS Football Rules Book, the NFHS makes no recommendation about the nature or extent of the modifications that may be appropriate for children who are younger or less skilled than high school varsity athletes.

Every individual using the NFHS football rules is responsible for prudent judgment with respect to each contest, athlete and facility, and each athlete is responsible for exercising caution and good sportsmanship. The NFHS football rules should be interpreted and applied so as to make reasonable accommodations for athletes, coaches and game officials with disabilities.

**2023 High School Football Rules Simplified & Illustrated**

Copyright © 2023 by the National Federation of State High School Associations with the United States Copyright Office.

Produced by Referee Enterprises Inc., publishers of Referee magazine.

Published by the
NATIONAL FEDERATION
OF STATE HIGH SCHOOL ASSOCIATIONS
PO Box 690
Indianapolis, IN 46206
Phone: 317-972-6900, Fax: 317-822-5700
www.nfhs.org

ISBN-13: 978-1-58208-556-2
Printed in the United States of America

# Table of Contents

Each state high school association adopting the NFHS football rules is the sole and exclusive source of binding rules interpretations for contests involving its member schools. Any person having questions about the interpretation of NFHS football rules should contact the rules interpreter designated by the respective state high school association.

The NFHS is the sole and exclusive source of model interpretations of NFHS football rules. State rules interpreters may contact the NFHS for model football rules interpretations. No other model football rules interpretations should be considered.

# 2023 NFHS Football Rules Changes

| Rule Changed | Rule Change Description |
|---|---|
| 1-5-3a(5)a 4, 5 (NEW) . . . . . . . . . . . | Clarified that towels do not have to be the same solid color for each player. |
| 2-29-1 . . . . . . . . . . . . . . . . . . . . . . . | Clarified when a player is inbounds after being out of bounds. |
| 2-32-16d (NEW), 9-4-3g . . . . . . . . . . | Added a list of criteria to help identify players who should be defined as defenseless receivers. |
| 7-5-2d EXCEPTION 2a, c (NEW), TABLE 7-5-2 d EXCEPTION 2a, c (NEW), TABLE 7-5 (1)d EXCEPTION 2a, c (NEW) . . . . . . . . . . . . . . . | Changed intentional grounding exception. |
| TABLE 7-5 2c (DELETED), 7-5 PENALTY . . . . . . . . . . . . . . . . . | Removed "intentional" from pass interference in TABLE 7-5. |
| 10-4, TABLE 10-4 (NEW), 10-6 (DELETED) . . . . . . . . . . . . . . . . . | Changes in basic spot penalty enforcement. |
| Six-Player – Rule 7g (NEW) . . . . | Clarification on the ball being handed forward on a running play. |

# 2023 Football Editorial Changes

1-1-7; 1-1-9; 1-3-2; 1-3-7 NOTE; TABLE 1-7; 1-8 (NEW); 3-6-1b(1); TABLE 7-5 (1) d EXCEPTION 2; 9-5-1; 9-8-1; FOOTBALL FUNDAMENTALS – II-5, X-3, X-5; RESOLVING TIED GAMES – 3-1; NINE-, EIGHT- AND SIX-PLAYER RULES DIFFERENCES – RULES 2 and 7; PENALTY SUMMARY; INDEX.

# 2023 Football Points of Emphasis

1. Helping the runner
2. Communication Between Coaches and Game Officials
3. Game Management

# Part 1

## 2023 New or Revised NFHS Rules

This simplified and illustrated book is a supplement to the 2023 NFHS Football Rules Book. As such, it is intended to aid in the administration of the game and in the standardization of interpretations through a unique method of presenting rules.

Each year the NFHS Football Rules Committee considers many items which are submitted as potential changes or revisions. The items which were approved by the NFHS Board of Directors are listed on page 6. The majority of illustrations in Part 1 show those changes and revisions.

The NFHS Football Rules Committee also identified areas of concern which are designated as "Point of Emphasis" for the current season. It appears in Part 2.

The illustrations found in Part 3 of this book have been revised to reflect any changes or clarifications as directed by the NFHS Football Rules Committee. Recent interpretations have been added to keep the contents current.

**1-5-3a(5)a 4, 5 (NEW)** It is legal for a player to have one moisture-absorbing solid-colored towel that has no more than one visible manufacturer's logo/trademark reference that does not exceed 2¼ square inches and does not exceed 2¼ inches in any dimension; and has no more than one school logo/trademark reference that does not exceed 2¼ square inches and does not exceed 2¼ inches in any dimension. Towels do not have to be the same solid color for each player.

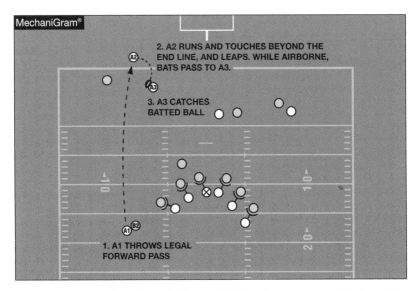

2. A2 RUNS AND TOUCHES BEYOND THE
END LINE, AND LEAPS. WHILE AIRBORNE,
BATS PASS TO A3.

3. A3 CATCHES
BATTED BALL

1. A1 THROWS LEGAL
FORWARD PASS

**2-29-1** A2 is out of bounds as he has not had any body part touch inbounds. Therefore, when A2 touches the ball after being out of bounds, he has caused the ball to become dead. The pass is incomplete and A2 is guilty of illegal participation.

**2-32-16d (NEW), 9-4-3g** The receiver is not defenseless because the opponent is attempting to tackle by wrapping arm(s) around the receiver.

PlayPic®

**2-32-16d (NEW), 9-4-3g** The receiver is not defenseless even if the contact by the opponent is forceful because the contact is initiated with open hands. The contact could be pass interference, however.

**2-32-16d (NEW), 9-4-3g** The receiver is not defenseless because of the incidental contact as a result of the defender making a play on the ball.

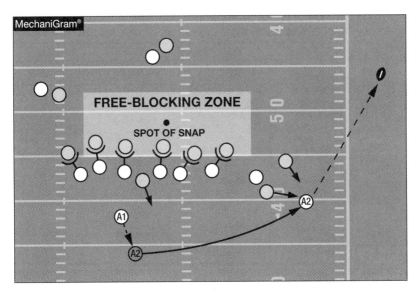

**7-5-2d EXCEPTION 2 (NEW), TABLE 7-5-2, TABLE 7-5** Foul for intentional grounding. The player taking advantage of the exception must be the player who received the snap.

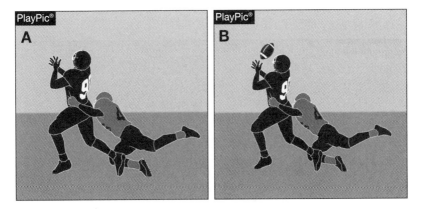

**TABLE 7-5 2c (DELETED), 7-5 PENALTY** The additional penalty for intentional pass interference as illustrated in PlayPic A has been deleted. The Team B player in the gray jersey will be penalized 15 yards for the pass interference foul committed in PlayPic B.

## SUMMARY OF MANY FOULS THAT CAN OCCUR DURING RUNNING PLAYS AND THEIR PENALTIES AND BASIC SPOTS UNLESS OTHERWISE SPECIFIED BY RULE

| FOUL BY | SPOT OF FOUL | END OF PLAY | BASIC SPOT | REFERENCE |
|---------|--------------|-------------|------------|-----------|
| A | Behind Line of Scrimmage | Behind Line of Scrimmage | Previous Spot | 10-4-2d |
| A | Behind Line of Scrimmage | Beyond Line of Scrimmage | Previous Spot | 10-4-2e |
| A | Beyond Line of Scrimmage | Behind Line of Scrimmage | Previous Spot | 10-4-2f |
| A | Beyond Line of Scrimmage | Beyond Line of Scrimmage | Foul Behind End of Run or Related Run – Spot of Foul | 10-4-4d |
| A | Beyond Line of Scrimmage | Beyond Line of Scrimmage | Foul Advance of End of Run or Related Run – Succeeding Spot | 10-4-5e |
| B | Behind Line of Scrimmage | Behind Line of Scrimmage | Previous Spot | 10-4-2d |
| B | Behind Line of Scrimmage | Beyond Line of Scrimmage | Succeding spot | 10-4-5f |
| B | Beyond Line of Scrimmage | Behind Line of Scrimmage | Previous spot | 10-4-2d |
| B | Beyond Line of Scrimmage | Beyond Previous Spot | Succeeding spot | 10 4-5f |
| B | Beyond Line of Scrimmage | Beyond Line of Scrimmage | Succeeding Spot | 10-4-5f |

**NOTE:** The basic spot is the spot of the foul when A commits any foul in his end zone for which the penalty is accepted (8-5-2c).

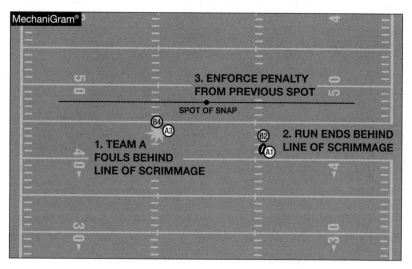

MechaniGram®

3. ENFORCE PENALTY FROM PREVIOUS SPOT

SPOT OF SNAP

1. TEAM A FOULS BEHIND LINE OF SCRIMMAGE

2. RUN ENDS BEHIND LINE OF SCRIMMAGE

**10-4-2d** The basic spot is the previous spot for a foul by A when the run or related run ends behind the line of scrimmage where there is no change of possession.

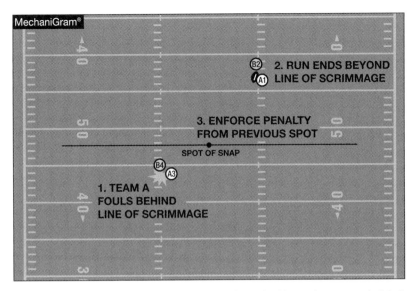

**2. RUN ENDS BEYOND LINE OF SCRIMMAGE**

**3. ENFORCE PENALTY FROM PREVIOUS SPOT**

SPOT OF SNAP

**1. TEAM A FOULS BEHIND LINE OF SCRIMMAGE**

**10-4-2e** The basic spot is the previous spot for a foul by A that occurs behind the line of scrimmage when the run or related run ends beyond the line of scrimmage.

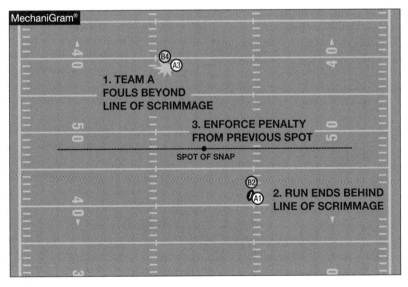

**1. TEAM A FOULS BEYOND LINE OF SCRIMMAGE**

**3. ENFORCE PENALTY FROM PREVIOUS SPOT**

SPOT OF SNAP

**2. RUN ENDS BEHIND LINE OF SCRIMMAGE**

**10-4-2f** The basic spot is the previous spot for a foul that occurs beyond the line of scrimmage when the run or related run ends behind the line of scrimmage.

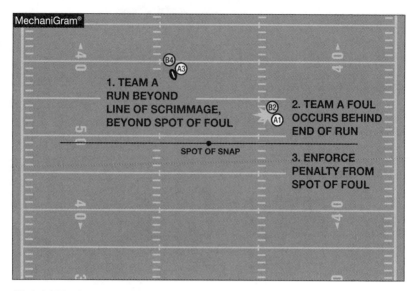

1. TEAM A RUN BEYOND LINE OF SCRIMMAGE, BEYOND SPOT OF FOUL

2. TEAM A FOUL OCCURS BEHIND END OF RUN

3. ENFORCE PENALTY FROM SPOT OF FOUL

SPOT OF SNAP

**10-4-4d** The basic spot is the spot of the foul by A that occurs beyond the line of scrimmage during a running play as defined in 10-3-2 when the run or related run ends beyond the line of scrimmage and the foul occurs behind the end of the run or related run.

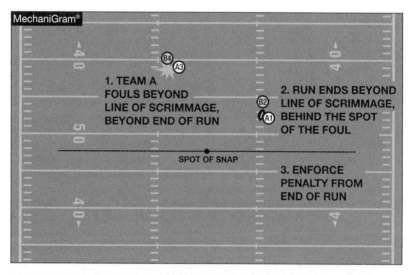

1. TEAM A FOULS BEYOND LINE OF SCRIMMAGE, BEYOND END OF RUN

2. RUN ENDS BEYOND LINE OF SCRIMMAGE, BEHIND THE SPOT OF THE FOUL

3. ENFORCE PENALTY FROM END OF RUN

SPOT OF SNAP

**10-4-5e** The basic spot is the spot of the foul for a foul by A that occurs beyond the line of scrimmage during a running play as defined in 10-3-2 when the run or related run ends beyond the line of scrimmage and the foul occurs in advance of the end of the run or related run.

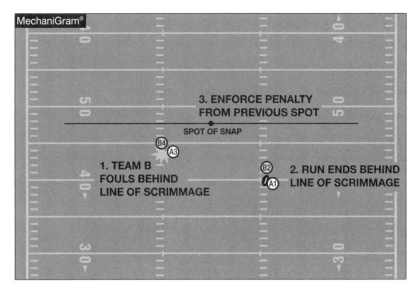

**10-4-2d** The basic spot is the previous spot for a foul by B when the run or related run ends behind the line of scrimmage where there is no change of possession.

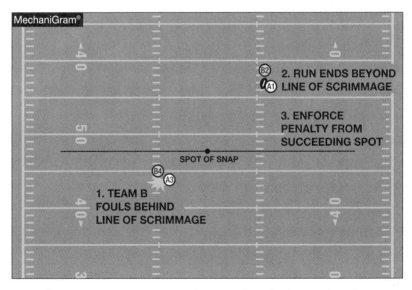

**10-4-5f** The basic spot is the succeeding spot for a foul by B when the run or related run ends beyond the line of scrimmage.

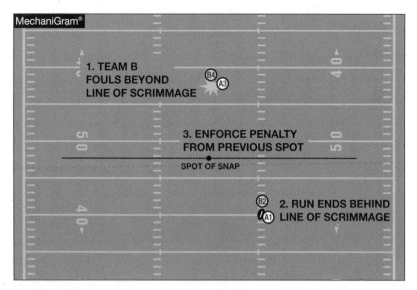

MechaniGram®

1. TEAM B
FOULS BEYOND
LINE OF SCRIMMAGE

3. ENFORCE PENALTY
FROM PREVIOUS SPOT

SPOT OF SNAP

2. RUN ENDS BEHIND
LINE OF SCRIMMAGE

**10-4-2d** The basic spot is the previous spot for a foul by B when the run or related run ends behind the line of scrimmage where there is no change of possession.

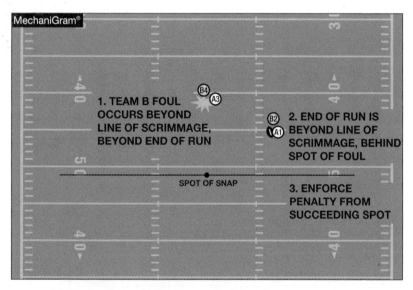

MechaniGram®

1. TEAM B FOUL
OCCURS BEYOND
LINE OF SCRIMMAGE,
BEYOND END OF RUN

2. END OF RUN IS
BEYOND LINE OF
SCRIMMAGE, BEHIND
SPOT OF FOUL

SPOT OF SNAP

3. ENFORCE
PENALTY FROM
SUCCEEDING SPOT

**10-4-5f** The basic spot is the succeeding spot for a foul by B when the run or related run ends beyond the line of scrimmage and the foul occurs beyond the end of the run.

**SIX-PLAYER – 7g (NEW)** A direct forward handoff may be made during a scrimmage down before a change of possession, provided both players are in or behind the neutral zone unless it is to the snapper.

# Part 2

## 2023 NFHS Points of Emphasis

### HELPING THE RUNNER

Rule changes have been made at higher levels of football allowing offensive teams to pile in behind and directly push the runner. Because of these changes, we are now seeing similar plays at the high school level. As guardians of the game, it is imperative that all stakeholders work together to remove "helping the runner" from our high school game.

Administrators, coaches and football game officials all have a responsibility to know, respect and teach/enforce the NFHS rules of high school football. Football is a vigorous, physical contact game and, for this reason, much attention is given to minimizing risk of injury to all players. Each respective rules code (NFL, NCAA and NFHS) has rules that coincide with the physical development of competing athletes and their goals for the game.

The NFHS Football Rules Committee's main focus is risk minimization, followed closely by assurance of a balance between offensive and defensive rules. Because the players on defense must guard against the pass, they are not able to counter the advantages created by "helping the runner" formations. Allowing teams to help the runner by illegal techniques swings the balance heavily in favor of the offense.

Football game officials need to change their view of "helping the runner" to a risk issue (clipping, chop block) and remove it from the "pioneer call" category and refocus on ending plays when forward progress is stopped. Pushing the pile is legal; direct contact and pushing, pulling, lifting of the runner is not.

The NFHS Coaches Code of Ethics states: "Coaches shall master the contest rules and shall teach the rules to their team members. Coaches shall not seek an advantage by circumvention of the spirit or letter of the rules. Coaches have a tremendous influence, for good or ill, on the education of the student, and thus shall never place the value of winning above the value of instilling the highest ideals of character."

If school administrators/athletic directors truly believe that activities are an extension of the classroom, they must be actively involved with programs they supervise and redirect coaches when they observe them teaching prohibited tactics.

Removing "helping the runner" from high school football will at times be met with resistance. School administrative support of football game officials, re-focus of coaches and education of players will lead to a smooth transition. All those directly involved in our great game must stay committed to trying to minimize risk to all players and maintaining the balance between offensive and defensive play.

## COMMUNICATION BETWEEN COACHES AND GAME OFFICIALS

Coaches and game officials must demonstrate respect for one another. This mutual appreciation is the foundation of appropriate and professional communication.

Football is an emotional game. Coaches and game officials must realize that competition often leads to intense interactions on the field. Both must work together and strive to manage verbal and nonverbal exchanges in ways that avoid escalating conflict.

Game officials must recognize their role in the game: to provide a service to the coaches and student-athletes in an unemotional and impartial manner. Game officials must always be respectful and maintain a calm demeanor in their comments to coaches, especially when tension is high. Game officials must avoid the urge to argue with coaches who disagree with their decisions. Coaches may ask questions, and game officials should make every effort to be approachable, actively listen, and provide correct and complete answers as soon as possible. Game officials should aim to be direct and concise in their communication of essential information.

When emotions are running especially high, game officials should de-escalate tensions and demonstrate empathy and understanding of the coach's perspective. Game officials must anticipate circumstances where coaches may become upset and pre-emptively diffuse the situation. A game official should never threaten the coach with consequences for their behavior, nor should a game official become defensive. If a coach exhibits inappropriate behavior and "crosses a line," the game official may choose to penalize the coach for unsportsmanlike conduct. However, throwing a flag should be a last resort. A better approach is to clearly and calmly tell the coach that the comments or behavior are unacceptable, and that it's difficult to focus on the on-field action if the coach continues to distract the game official.

Coaches model acceptable and unacceptable behavior for their student-athletes. If coaches disrespect game officials and make derogatory comments, players will behave in the same way. Coaches should win with grace and lose with dignity. Coaches must understand that the football field is an extension of the classroom and must exhibit proper conduct. This includes respecting the decisions of game officials even when they disagree, and handling differences of opinion in a civil and dignified manner. Dialogue with game officials should be constructive and respectful, not confrontational. Handling disagreements in a business-like manner teaches players good sportsmanship, which is a perennial focus of the NFHS.

Coaches and game officials have a professional responsibility to demonstrate respect for one another and communicate appropriately. Coaches and game officials love the game and desire to positively impact young people. Proper communication during competition teaches players a valuable life lesson about conflict resolution.

## GAME MANAGEMENT

Each school community must take pride in hosting an athletic contest or event. Proper advance planning is key to an orderly, secure, safe and enjoyable activity. Planning begins with clearly defined tasks for game administration and event personnel. Beginning with the arrival of players, game officials and spectators, each school must have a purposeful plan to address any and all expected issues, as well as the unforeseen.

Preparation begins with clear and concise communication between the host and the competing school regarding the logistics of arrival and departure. Meeting and greeting the visiting team is certainly the beginning of good sportsmanship. Clearly communicated information, such as parking information, location of ticket booths and entry gates, when given to the visitors is another step in assuring a great experience for all participants.

Game officials should be afforded the same communication considerations given the visiting school community. Host administration must provide accurate information for the officiating crew so as to ease any pre-game apprehension or uncertainty. Clear, concise communication is of utmost importance. Having assigned personnel to greet game officials and address all their pre-game and post-game needs is a bare minimum for the host school. Security of game officials must be an absolute priority. Make sure the locker room is properly supervised and access is limited to proper personnel only.

During the game, security of game personnel begins with ensuring that the sideline is properly secured and the playing field is restricted to essential game personnel. For safety and security reasons, essential game personnel would include game participants, reporters, photographers and game administration. All other, non-essential personnel should be located in the bleachers. All non-participants on the event level should be credentialed and restricted to being no closer than 2 yards from the sideline. Game officials are responsible for securing the team boxes and coaches' area. Sideline management begins with the consistent enforcement of game rules pertaining to the restricted area and the team box. The restricted area is designated to make the sidelines safe for all participants and to give game officials ample space to work. Game administration should be alert to requests of game officials in addressing problems beyond the team box and coaches' area.

The conduct of non-participants is the domain of game and school administration. Expectations for the behavior of spectators and other attendees should be clearly, and repeatedly, communicated to all attendees. The reading of a sportsmanship script before the game is one method of communicating expectations. Good sportsmanship must become part of the culture of any school community. Behavior not acceptable in the school's hallways should not be acceptable on the courts or playing fields.

Appropriate conduct of the public-address announcer is vital to the game atmosphere. The public-address announcer must be the first line of sportsmanship and must exemplify expected and acceptable conduct. The goal of the public-address announcer is to inform and not entertain. Giving play-by-play of game action and/or critiquing game officials is unacceptable. The public-address announcer must be positive and respectful to all involved in the game.

## MINIMAL GAME ADMINISTRATION EXPECTATIONS

- Clearly communicated event itinerary
- Required field markings and game equipment
- Clock operator(s)
- Line-to-gain crew
- Game official accommodations
- Visiting team accommodations
- Support personnel
- Medical personnel
- Security personnel
- Hospitality for game personnel and administration, inclusive of game officials

# Part 3
## Rule 1

## The Game, Field, Players and Equipment

The origin of the game of football is not clear. Football, as played in the United States, is a blend of soccer and rugby, with other variations making it a truly unique sport. Football is played with an inflated ball by two teams of 11 players each on a rectangular field 360 by 160 feet. The specific lines and marks are found in the NFHS Football Rules Book.

Player equipment has a double purpose. It must protect the wearer and also other players against the dangers of unnecessary injury. The rules are constantly reviewed and often revised to allow use of new equipment which has been developed to provide greater protection to the participants. It is the responsibility of the rules committee to specify equipment to protect players whether on offense or defense. Because past rules committees have met this responsibility, there has been a continuous improvement in football player equipment.

The game is administered by game officials whose duties are outlined in the NFHS Football Rules Book and NFHS Football Game Officials Manual. Game officials must accept the responsibility of enforcing the letter, as well as the spirit, of the rules promptly and consistently. The risk minimization of all players is paramount and with this there can be no compromise. A thorough study and understanding of all the NFHS football publications is necessary to meet this responsibility.

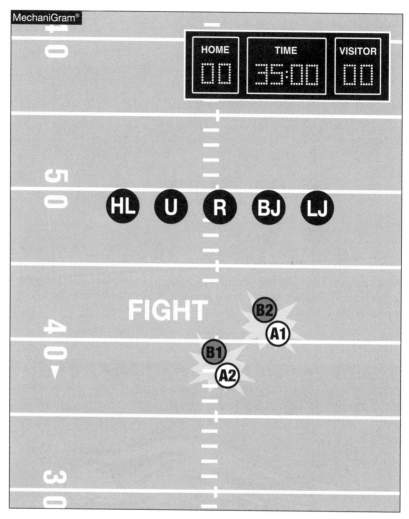

**1-1-7** Game officials have authority if a state association has a policy that game officials' authority begins more than 30 minutes before the game.

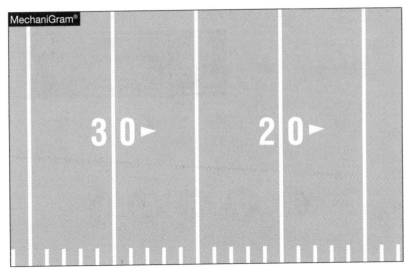

**1-2-3a** Lines shall be marked with a noncaustic, nontoxic material designed for marking fields such as powdered gypsum, calcium carbonate and liquid aerosol paint. It is recommended that these lines be white.

**1-2-3b NOTE 2** If the field of play has a logo in the center or at any other part of the field of play, that logo shall not obstruct the visibility of the required marks every five yards. This logo would not be legal and should be reported to the state association after the game.

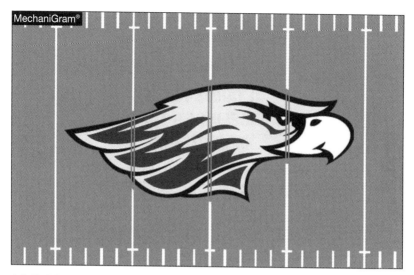

**1-2-3b NOTE 2** A solid or shadow-bordered 4-inch wide line is permissible A shadow line is a line that designates the required 4-inch width by use of a border or outline lines at least ¼-inch wide, which shall lie within the 4-inch width. Shadow lines that are the natural color of the field of play are permissible. The area within these lines need not be one color, but the continuous 4-inch wide outline must be clearly visible to the game officials.

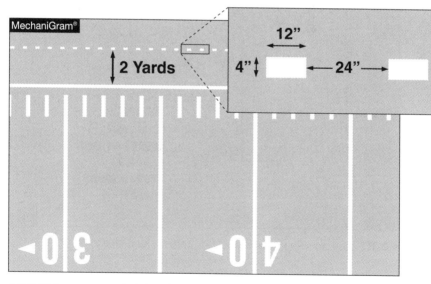

**1-2-3d** It is recommended that the restraining line be marked by placing 12-inch-long lines, separated at 24-inch intervals.

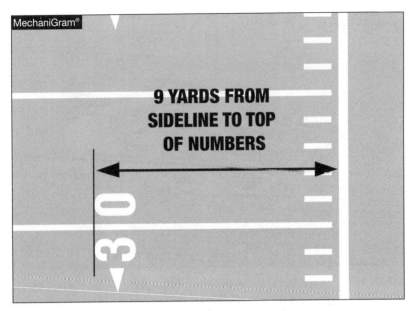

**9 YARDS FROM SIDELINE TO TOP OF NUMBERS**

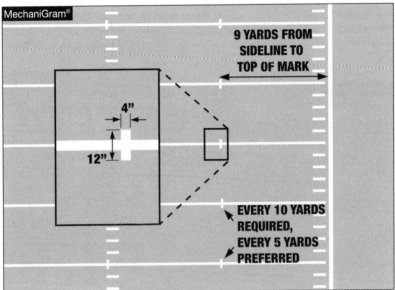

**9 YARDS FROM SIDELINE TO TOP OF MARK**

4"

12"

**EVERY 10 YARDS REQUIRED, EVERY 5 YARDS PREFERRED**

**1-2-3f** 9-yard marks or numbers are required for all fields.

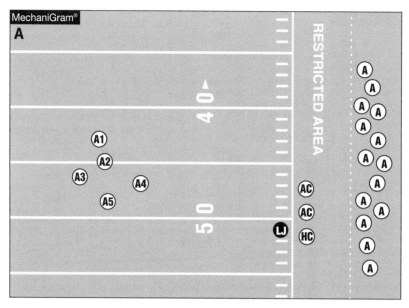

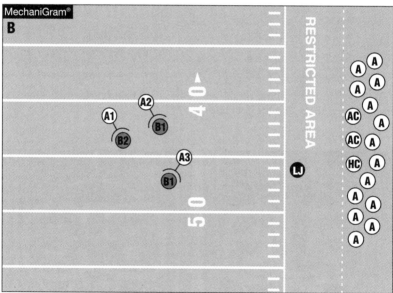

**1-2-3g; 9-8-3** When the ball is dead, a maximum of three coaches may be in the restricted area (MechaniGram A). Once the ball is snapped, no nonplayer may be in the restricted area (MechaniGram B). The first offense results in a team warning; the second offense, a five-yard penalty for sideline interference; and subsequent offenses, 15 yards for unsportsmanlike conduct charged to the head coach. The two-yard restricted area may only be used when the ball is dead.

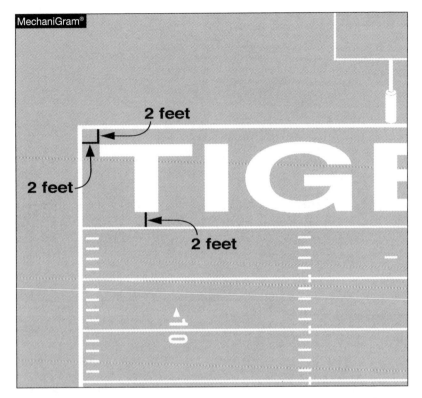

**1-2-3h** Decorative markings in the end zones shall be no closer than 2 feet from the boundary and the goal lines.

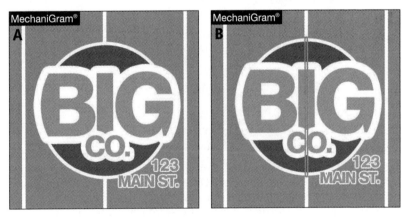

**1-2-3l** Advertising and/or commercial markings shall not obstruct the yard lines, hash marks or 9-yard marks. The logo in MechaniGram A is illegal, but the one in MechaniGram B is legal.

**1-3-1c** A legal football has a continuous 1-inch white or yellow stripe centered 3 to 3¼ inches from each end of the ball free from decorations or logos added during or after production. The stripes shall be located only on the two panels adjacent to the laces (PlayPic A). Footballs with a continuous solid white or yellow stripes ⅜ inch wide running parallel to and ¼ inch from each side of each seam to 1 inch from the laces (PlayPic B) are not allowed.

**1-3-1h** The ball may contain only the following permissible items: Ball manufacturer's name and/or logo; School name, logo and/or mascot; Conference name and/or logo; State association name and/or logos; and NFHS name and/or logos.

**1-3-2** It is permissible for either team to have an additional ball(s) approved during the course of the game. When weather conditions change it is often necessary to use a different ball. In normal situations the referee will approve and mark the balls before game time.

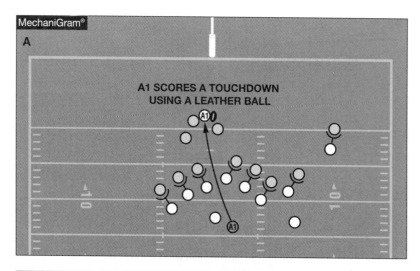

**MechaniGram®**

**A**

A1 SCORES A TOUCHDOWN
USING A LEATHER BALL

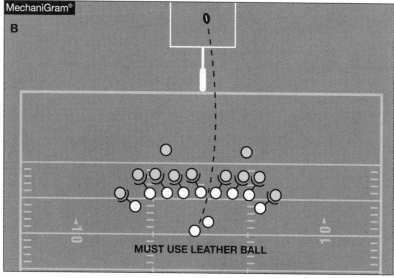

**MechaniGram®**

**B**

MUST USE LEATHER BALL

**1-3-3** Any game official may order the ball changed between downs. Unless the ball is ordered changed by the Referee or another game official, Team A scoring a touchdown with one ball (MechaniGram A) may not request a different ball for the try (MechaniGram B) but may use a different approved ball for the ensuing free kick (PlayPic C).

**PlayPic®**

**C**

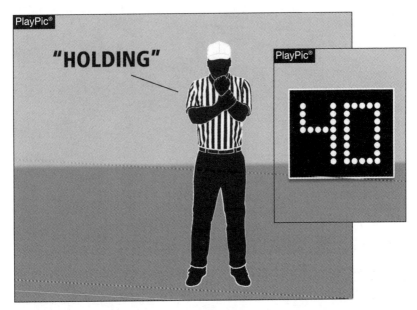

**"HOLDING"**

**1-3-7** State associations may authorize use of supplementary equipment to aid in game administration. The microphone on the referee and the 40-second play clock are just two examples of equipment which can be used when properly authorized.

**1-3-7 NOTE; TABLE 1-7 — 1-3-7 NOTE (6)** By adoption, state associations may create instant replay procedures that permit game or replay officials to use a replay monitor during state postseason games to determine if a decision by the on-field game officials is incorrect.

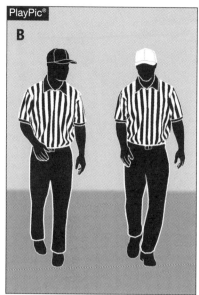

**1-4-1, 1-4-4, 2-32-5, 3-5-2, 10-1-1, 10-1-2, 10-2-4** Prior to the game the head coach will notify the referee of the designated representative (coach or player) who will make decisions regarding penalty acceptance or declination (PlayPic A). When a foul occurs, the head linesman or line judge will inform the referee as to the penalty decision if the coach is the decision maker (PlayPic B).

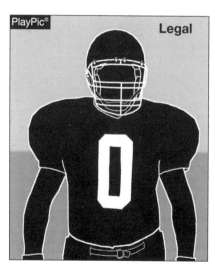

**1-4-2, 1-4-3, 7-2-5b EXCEPTIONS, 7-5-6a** Each player shall be numbered 0 though 99 inclusive. Any number preceded by the digit zero such as "00" is illegal.

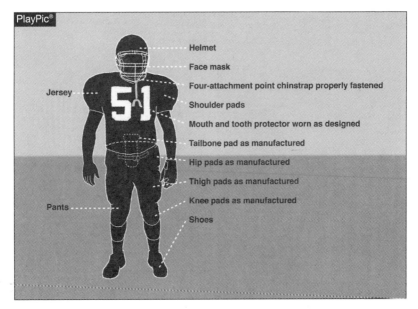

PlayPic®

Helmet

Face mask

Four-attachment point chinstrap properly fastened

Jersey

Shoulder pads

Mouth and tooth protector worn as designed

Tailbone pad as manufactured

Hip pads as manufactured

Thigh pads as manufactured

Knee pads as manufactured

Pants

Shoes

**1-5-1** The items of equipment shown must be worn by all players. A player may not participate unless he or she is wearing all required equipment which is professionally manufactured and not altered to decrease protection.

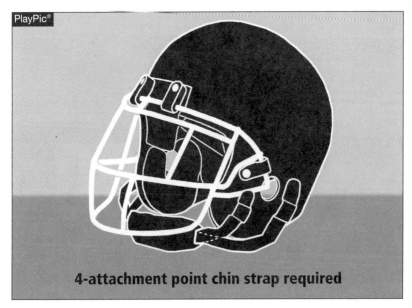

PlayPic®

**4-attachment point chin strap required**

**1-5-1a(2)** The helmet shall be secured by a properly fastened chin strap with at least four attachment points.

**1-5-1a NOTE** All players shall wear helmets that carry a warning label regarding the risk of injury and a manufacturer's or reconditioner's certification indicating satisfaction of NOCSAE standards. All such reconditioned helmets shall show recertification to indicate satisfaction with the NOCSAE standard. The coach's pregame verification to the referee and another game official that all players are properly equipped in compliance with the rules includes the exterior warning label.

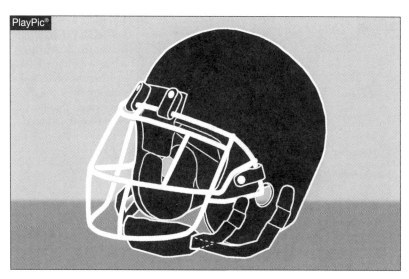

**1-5-1a(1)** A helmet and face mask which met the NOCSAE standard at the time of manufacture. The face mask shall have a surface covered with resilient material designed to prevent chipping, burrs or abrasiveness and be properly secured to the helmet as designed by the manufacturer.

**LINE JUDGE**

**1-5-1a(2) NOTE; 1-5-4** A crew member other than the umpire may accompany the referee to the pregame meeting with the head coaches, during which the coach verifies his team is legally equipped. Any questions regarding legality of a player's equipment shall be resolved by the umpire.

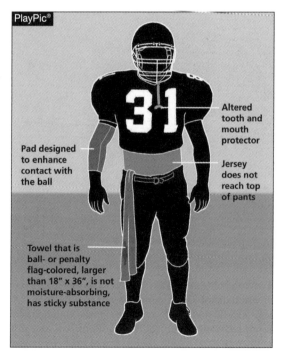

Altered tooth and mouth protector

Pad designed to enhance contact with the ball

Jersey does not reach top of pants

Towel that is ball- or penalty flag-colored, larger than 18" x 36", is not moisture-absorbing, has sticky substance

**1-5-1b(1); 1-5-3a(5)a; 1-5-3c(5); 1-5-3c(9)** No player may participate while wearing illegal equipment, an illegal uniform or with equipment that has been illegally altered.

**1-5-1b(3)** The home jersey is to be a dark color that clearly contrasts with white. The home jersey on the left is legal. The home jersey on the right is illegal.

**1-5-1(b)3** The home team jerseys in the PlayPic are illegal. NOTE: Rules 1-5-1b(2)e and 1-5-1b(3)e: The visiting team is responsible for avoidance of similarity of colors, but if there is doubt, the referee may require players of the home team to change jerseys.

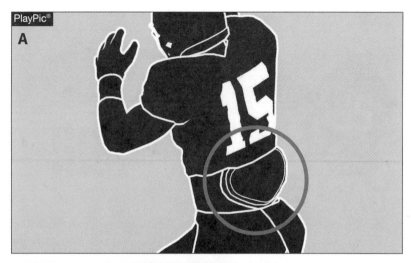

**1-5-1b(1)** The jersey must completely cover all pads worn above the waist on the torso, such as the back pad in PlayPic A, and the shoulder pad as seen in PlayPic B.

**1-5-1b(2a), (3a)** Allowable adornments and accessory on the patterns on the jersey include the school's nickname, school logo, school name and/or player name within the body and/or on the shoulders.

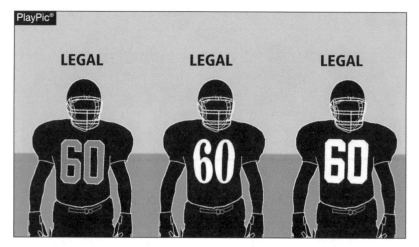

**1-5-1c** These jersey numerals are legal. Different styles of numerals also are legal as long as they are Arabic numbers 0 through 99 and they are clearly visible and legible. All players of one team must wear numbers identical in style front and back and no teammates may participate during the same down wearing identical numbers.

**1-5-1c(1); 1-5-1c(2)** The number on each jersey shall be clearly visible and legible. The jersey on the left is illegal because the number shall also be centered on the jersey horizontally, as in the jersey on the right.

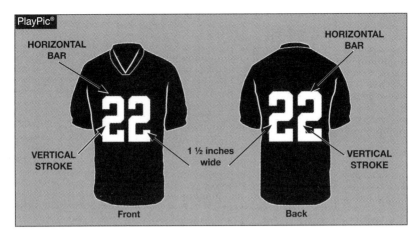

**1-5-1c; 1-5-1c(6)** The entire body of the number (the continuous horizontal bars and vertical strokes) exclusive of any border(s) shall be approximately 1½ inches wide. The requirements for the size of jersey numbers are in effect through the 2023 season. Also, effective in the 2024 season, jersey numbers must be a single solid color that clearly contrasts with the body color of the jersey.

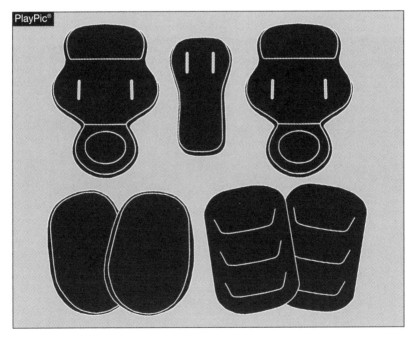

**1-5-1d(1); 1-5-1d(2); 1-5-1d(4)** Hip pads and tailbone protector, knee pads, and thigh guards must be unaltered from the manufacturer's original design/production.

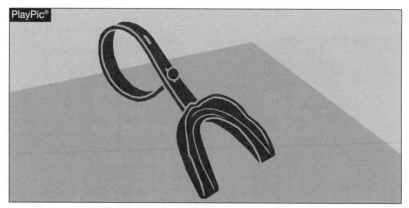

**1-5-1d(5)** A tooth and mouth protector (intraoral) which shall include an occlusal (protecting and separating the biting surfaces) portion and a labial (protecting the teeth and supporting structures) portion and covers the posterior teeth with adequate thickness is required. It is recommended the protector be properly fitted, protecting the anterior (leading) dental arch and constructed from a model made from an impression of the individual's teeth and constructed and fitted to the individual by impressing the teeth into the tooth and mouth protector itself.

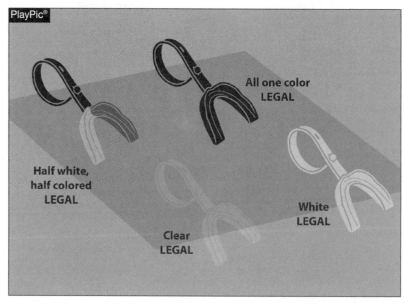

All one color
LEGAL

Half white,
half colored
LEGAL

White
LEGAL

Clear
LEGAL

**1-5-1d(5a)** Tooth and mouth protectors may be any color, including white or clear.

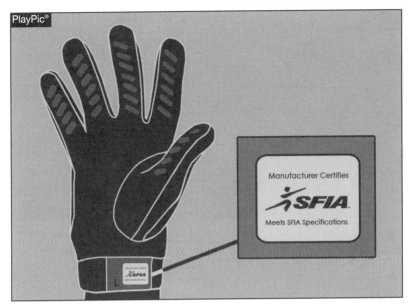

**1-5 NOTE; 1-5-2b** Gloves which meet the SFIA specification at the time of manufacture are legal. The stamp must be visible and appear legibly on the exterior wrist opening.

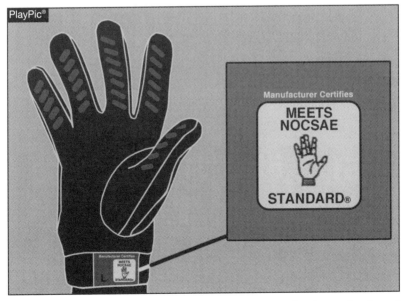

**1-5 NOTE; 1-5-2b** Gloves which meet the NOCSAE specification at the time of manufacture are legal. The stamp must be visible and appear legibly on the exterior wrist opening.

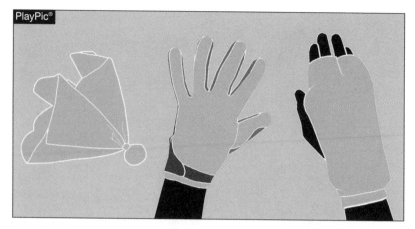

**1-5-3c(1)** Gloves and hand pads may not be the same color as penalty markers.

**1-5-3a(5)a** Towels shall not be ball- or penalty flag-colored. Not every player has to wear a towel (PlayPic A). Towels do not have to be the same solid color. The towels in PlayPic B are legal.

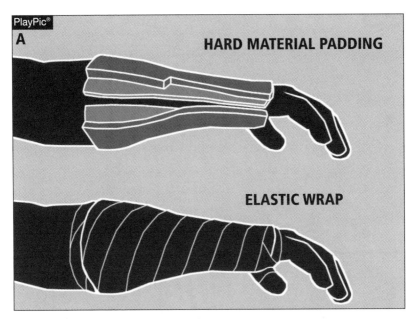

**HARD MATERIAL PADDING**

**ELASTIC WRAP**

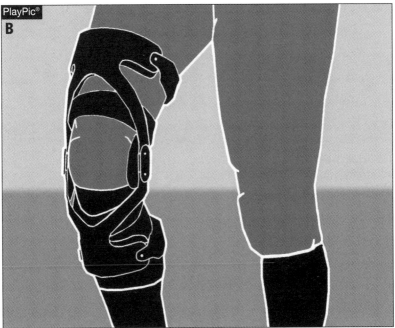

**1-5-3b(1); 1-5-3b(3)** Hard and unyielding items (guards, casts, braces, etc.) on the hand, wrist, forearm, elbow, or upper arm (PlayPic A) must be padded with a closed-cell, slow-recovery foam padding no less than one-half inch in thickness. Knee braces may not be worn on top of the pants (PlayPic B).

**1-5-3c(2); 1-6-1; 1-6-2** Electronic signage used to signal plays or other information from the sideline is illegal.

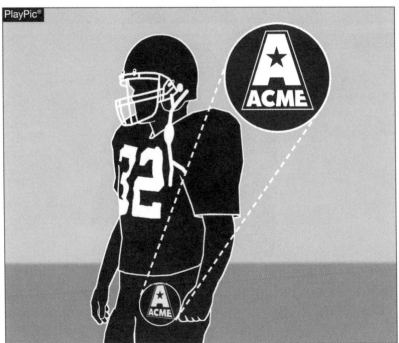

**1-5-3a(1)a; 1-5-3a(1)b** Jerseys/pants may have only one visible reference to the manufacturer and the reference on each may not exceed 2¼ square inches. The references shown are too large and would be illegal.

**1-5-3c(8)** If worn, play cards must be worn on the wrist or arm, as seen in PlayPic A. Play cards may not be attached to the belt (PlayPic B) or otherwise worn.

**1-5-3c(3)** If worn, eye shade (grease or no-glare strips or stickers) that is not a solid stroke or includes words, numbers, logos or other symbols within the eye shade is illegal. If a player uses eye shade, it must be applied using a single solid stroke under each eye. The eye shade shall be located below and within the width of the eye socket and not extend below the cheek bone.

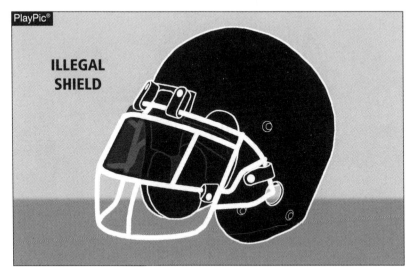

ILLEGAL
SHIELD

**1-5-3c(4)** If an eyeshield is worn, it must be constructed of a molded, rigid material that is clear without the presence of any tint. NOTE: Tinted eyewear worn on the face and under the face mask is legal.

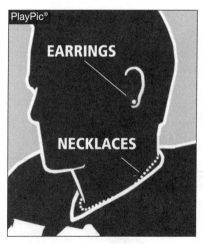

EARRINGS

NECKLACES

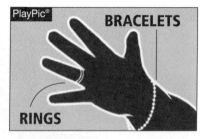

BRACELETS

RINGS

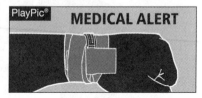

MEDICAL ALERT

**1-5-3c(6)** Jewelry such as earrings, necklaces, bracelets and rings shall not be worn. Religious and medical-alert medals are not considered jewelry. A religious medal must be taped and worn under the uniform. A medical-alert medal must be taped and may be visible.

**1-5-4** Prior to the game, the head coach shall be responsible for verifying to the referee and another game official that all of his players are legally equipped in compliance with NFHS football rules and will use no illegal equipment. Questions regarding legality of player equipment or presence of required equipment shall be resolved by the umpire.

**1-5-4, 1-5-5, 3-5-10e, 9-8-1h** The player in PlayPic A is not wearing required equipment during a down. There is no yardage penalty, but the player must be replaced for at least one down (PlayPic B) and may not return until he is wearing the required equipment.

**1-6** Electronic communication devices may be used by coaches and nonplayers on the sidelines as long as they are not used to communicate with players (PlayPic A). Electronic signage used to signal plays or other information from the sideline is illegal, as in PlayPic B.

**1-6** During an outside the 9-yard marks conference (PlayPic A), the coach may show players an electronic device. During an inside the 9-yard marks conference, a coach may use the device (PlayPic B) but not show it to players (PlayPic C).

**1-6-2** LAN phones and/or headsets may be used by coaches, other nonplayers and players; however, players may use LAN phones and/or headsets only during authorized outside 9-yard mark conferences.

**1-6-2** An authorized conference in front of the team box can be conducted as far onto the field as the 9-yard marks. Regardless if the conference takes place between the hash marks or within the 9-yard marks in front of the team box, a coach may use LAN phones or headphones.

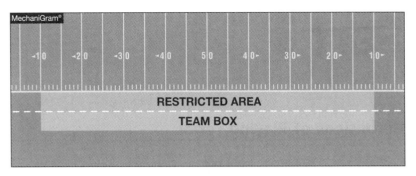

**1-7 (3.); 1-2-3g Notes 3.** It is permissible for state associations to approve an extension of the team box and to determine the individuals who may be in the extended area, provided such extension is the same for both teams.

**1-8** Each state association may, in keeping with applicable laws, authorize exceptions to NFHS playing rules to provide reasonable accommodations to individual participants with disabilities and/or special needs, as well as those individuals with unique and extenuating circumstances. The accommodations should not fundamentally alter the sport or heighten risk to the athlete/others or place opponents at a disadvantage.

# Part 3
## Rule 2

## Definitions of Playing Terms

Coaches and game officials have a tendency to overlook Rule 2, thinking that definitions are not as important as, for example, those situations dealing with various types of rules infractions and their respective penalties. Nothing could be further from the truth. Rule 2, indeed, is the most important rule in the book. A few examples of some basic definitions:

1. Batting is intentionally slapping or striking the ball with the arm or hand.

2. A catch is the act of establishing player possession of a live ball in flight.

3. Force is not a factor when a backward pass or fumble is declared dead in the end zone of the opponent of the player who passed or fumbled, with no player possession.

4. A fumble is any loss of player possession other than by legal kick, passing or handing.

5. The line of scrimmage for each team is a vertical plane through the point of the ball nearest the team's goal line.

6. The neutral zone is the space between the two free-kick lines during a free-kick down and between the two scrimmage lines during a scrimmage down.

A–refers to the offensive team that puts the ball in play during a scrimmage down. B–refers to their opponents, the defensive team. K–refers to the kicking team, while R–identifies the receiving team during a free or scrimmage kick. The offense is the team which is in possession. At such time, the opponent is the defense.

To fully understand the game, everyone concerned must have a complete understanding of the definitions. The definitions are clear and concise. Terms used in the definitions are unique and actually form the language of the game.

**2-3-2a** This is a legal blocking position with closed or cupped hands. The hands are in advance of the elbows and not extended more than 45 degrees from the body. The elbows may be either inside or outside the frame of the shoulders. The hands are closed or cupped with the palms not facing the opponents. The forearms may not be extended more than 45 degrees from the blocker's body. If they are, the hands must be open and shall not be locked.

**2-3-2b** This is a legal blocking position with extended arms and open hands. Team A blockers may use open hands when blocking if the hands are in advance of the elbows and within the blocker's frame and the opponent's frame. The hands must be open when the forearms are extended more than 45 degrees from the blocker's body.

PlayPic® A

PlayPic® B

PlayPic® C

**2-3-2b; 2-5-2** The PlayPics depict contact outside the free-blocking zone. The original contact in PlayPic A is legal (2-5-2). However, the opponent evades the blocker in PlayPic B. The blocker makes illegal contact on the back in PlayPic C. The block was not continuous and results in a block in the back foul in PlayPic C. If the blocker had maintained contact in PlayPic B the block would have been legal.

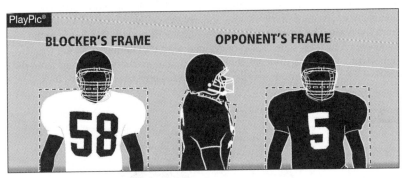

PlayPic®

BLOCKER'S FRAME          OPPONENT'S FRAME

58          5

**2-3-2b (2 & 3)** The frame of the blocker's body is the front of the body at or below the shoulders. The frame of the opponent's body is at the shoulders or below, other than the back.

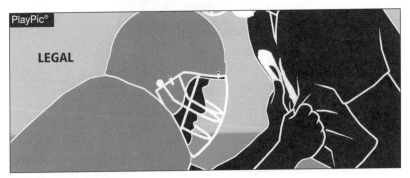

PlayPic®

LEGAL

**2-3-5b** Any defensive player (shown in gray) may use hands to get to a runner or loose ball as long as such contact is not pass interference, a personal foul or illegal use of hands.

**2-3-7, 2-17-1, 2-17-2, 9-3-2** The initial contact in PlayPic A is above the waist. In PlayPic B, the blocker then loses contact and the blocker starts a new block below the waist. This is a foul. A block below the waist is legal if it occurs in the free-blocking zone, provided both players were on their lines of scrimmage and within the zone at the time of the snap and the block is an immediate, initial action following the snap.

PlayPic® A

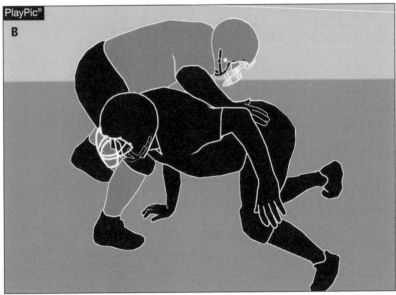

PlayPic® B

**2-3-7, 2-17-1, 2-17-2, 9-3-2** While in the free-blocking zone, the initial contact is with the hands below the waist (PlayPic A). When the blocker finishes the block below the waist (PlayPic B), it is not a foul. A block below the waist is legal if it occurs in the free-blocking zone, provided both players were on their lines of scrimmage and within the zone at the time of the snap and the block is an immediate, initial action following the snap.

PlayPic®

**2-3-7, 2-17-2, 9-3-2** The rules regarding blocking below the waist apply equally to both teams. When a defender goes below the waist outside the free-blocking zone to take out the lead blocker it is an illegal block by the defender. A block below the waist is only legal if it occurs in the free-blocking zone, provided both players were on their lines of scrimmage and within the zone at the time of the snap and the block is an immediate, initial action following the snap.

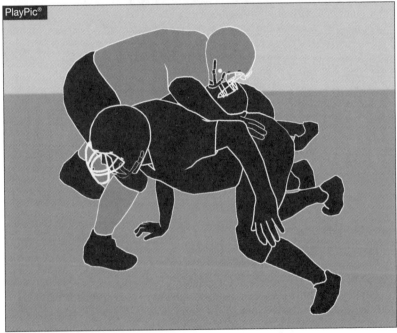

**2-3-8** Combination blocks in the free-blocking zone that consist of either two low blocks (at the knee or below) or two high blocks are legal.

PlayPic®

**2-3-8** A chop block is combination block by two or more teammates against an opponent other than the runner, with or without delay, where one of the blocks is below the waist and one of the blocks is above the waist.

PlayPic®

PlayPic®

**2-3-10; 9-4-3n; 9-4 PENALTY** A blindside block is a block against an opponent other than the runner, who does not see the blocker approaching.

**2-4-1** No catch. The receiver does not have possession of the ball inbounds when he comes down. When there is possession, the first foot to touch the ground determines whether it is a catch — as it must touch inbounds, even if the other foot then touches out of bounds. If the feet touch the ground simultaneously, both must be inbounds.

**2-4-1** A catch is the act of establishing player possession of a live ball which is in flight, and first contacting the ground inbounds while maintaining possession of the ball. Because the player's foot is inbounds when he grasps the ball (PlayPic A), and maintains possession after the contact and landing out of bounds (PlayPic B), it is a catch.

**2-4-1** The airborne player grasps the ball (PlayPic A), but after the contact by an opponent (PlayPic B), he lands out of bounds (PlayPic C). That is not a catch.

**2-4-1** In PlayPic A, the airborne receiver is contacted so that his forward progress is stopped. When the defender carries him out of bounds (PlayPic B), the result is a completed pass.

**2-4-1** When an airborne receiver is contacted by a defender (PlayPic A), causing him to make first contact with the ground out of bounds (PlayPic B), it is an incomplete pass. The game official's judgment regarding whether A1 would have landed inbounds is not a factor.

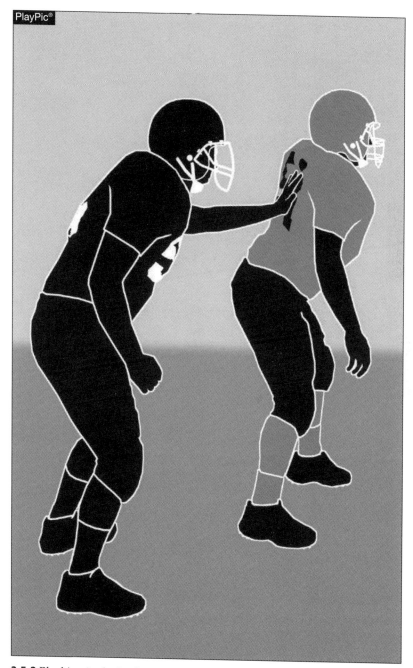

**2-5-2** Blocking in the back is against an opponent with the initial contact inside the shoulders, below the helmet and above the waist. The penalty for blocking in the back is 10 yards.

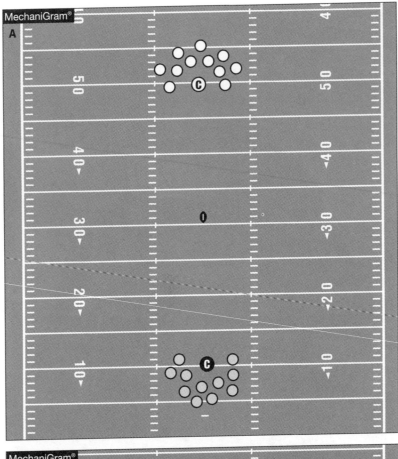

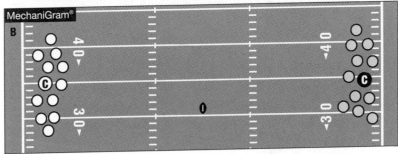

**2-6-1; 2-6-2** When a team's request for a charged team time-out is granted, the teams shall use one of two types of authorized team conferences. The "between 9-yard mark conferences" (MechaniGram A) involve one coach on the field to confer with no more than 11 players at his team's huddle between the 9-yard marks. The "outside 9-yard mark conference" (MechaniGram B) consists of one or more team members and one or more coaches directly in front of the team box within 9 yards of the sideline.

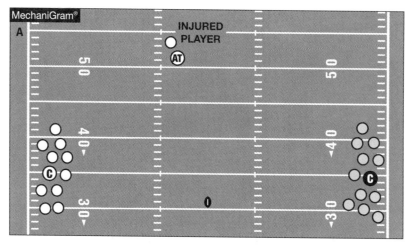

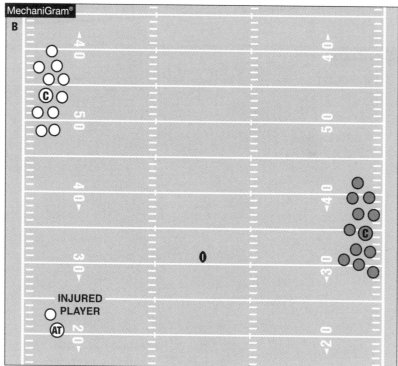

**2-6-1; 2-6-2** When an injury occurs and the referee grants an authorized conference, it must be an "outside 9-yard mark conference" (MechaniGram A). If the injured player is outside the 9-yard marks but in front of the team box, the conference must still be conducted outside the 9-yard marks and in front of the restricted area but away from the injured player (MechaniGram B). That will give medical personnel time and space to address the injured player.

**3-5-2a; 3-5-2a Note** If the head coach is not on the sideline, such as due to a disqualification (PlayPic A) or injury (PlayPic B), the head coach may designate someone to request time-outs from the sideline (PlayPic C). The designee shall remain in place for the entire game except in case of emergency.

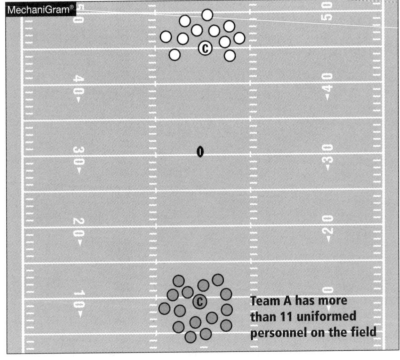

Team A has more than 11 uniformed personnel on the field

**2-6-2b** It is illegal to have more than 11 players meet with the coach for a conference between the 9-yard marks. The penalty is 15 yards (9-8-1f).

**2-9-1** The prohibition against contacting a player who has given a valid fair-catch signal ceases if the kick is muffed. When No. 80 catches the ball in Play Pic D, it is a fair catch. The contact in PlayPic C is not kick-catch interference. The captain may choose to snap or free kick anywhere between the hash marks on the yard line through the spot of the catch.

**2-9-4** A signal given after the kick has touched a receiver or after it has touched the ground is an invalid fair-catch signal. The ball becomes dead as soon as the kick is caught or recovered. The foul will be enforced as a post-scrimmage kick foul.

**2-11** Fighting is any attempt by a player or nonplayer to strike or engage a player or nonplayer in a combative manner unrelated to football. Included are attempts to strike with hand(s), arm(s), leg(s), feet or foot, whether or not there is contact. The four examples of fighting pictured all call for a 15-yard penalty and disqualification.

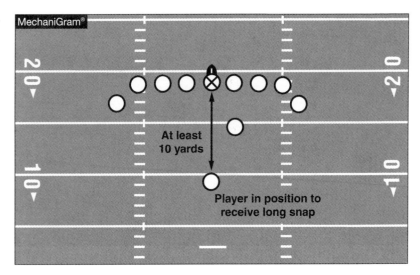

**2-14-2b** Legal scrimmage-kick formation. A member of the kicking team is 10 yards or more behind the line of scrimmage and in position to receive the long snap.

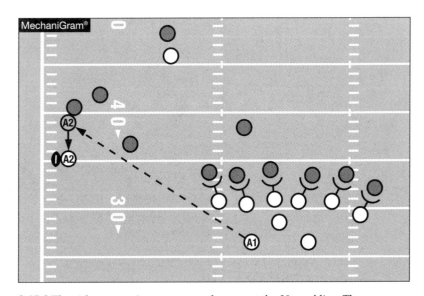

**2-15-2** The airborne receiver possesses the pass at the 39-yard line. The defensive contact causes him to be driven backward and the catch is completed well short of the 39 Since the defender caused the change in direction, forward progress is awarded to the farthest advancement after possessing the ball.

**B's END ZONE**

**2-15-2** Airborne receiver No. 5 possesses the ball beyond the plane of B's goal line. The defensive contact forces No. 5 out of the end zone and the catch is completed in the field of play No. 5 is given forward progress at the point of possession and it is a touchdown.

**2-16-2c** Any single flagrant foul results in disqualification of the offender. Among the acts that may be considered flagrant are violent and repeated pulls on a face mask (PlayPic A), intentional contact of a game official (PlayPic B) and prolonged taunting of an opponent (PlayPic C).

**2-16-2e; 10-2-4** It is a multiple foul when two or more live-ball fouls (other than nonplayer or unsportsmanlike) are committed during the same down by the same team (PlayPic A). One penalty must be declined (PlayPic B) as only one may be enforced (PlayPic C).

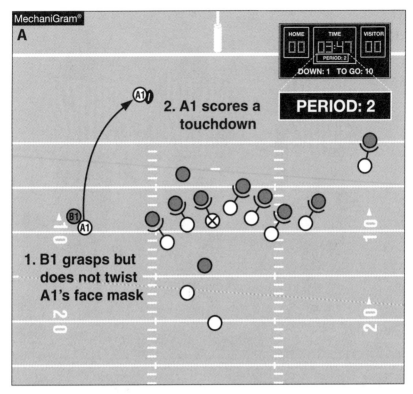

**MechaniGram®**

**A**

2. A1 scores a touchdown

PERIOD: 2

1. B1 grasps but does not twist A1's face mask

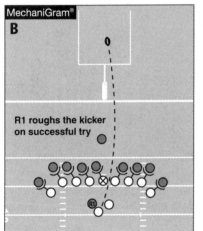

**MechaniGram®**

**B**

R1 roughs the kicker on successful try

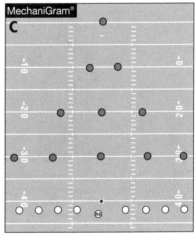

**MechaniGram®**

**C**

**2-16-2e; 8-2-2; 10-2-4** The opponent of the scoring team commits a live-ball foul (other than unsportmanlike conduct or a nonplayer foul) during a down in which there was no change of possession (MechaniGram A). The same team commits a live-ball foul during the try (MechaniGram B). Both penalties may be enforced on the subsequent kickoff (MechaniGram C).

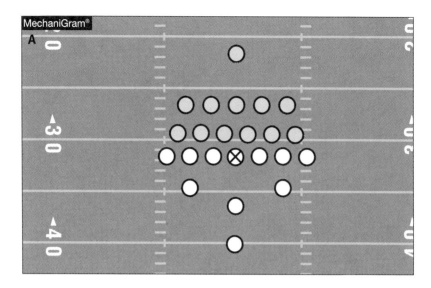

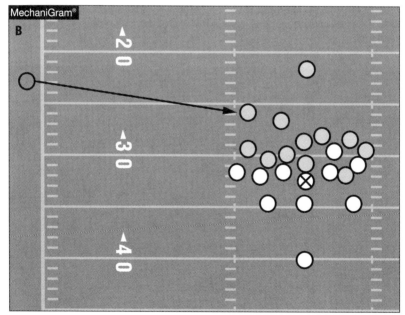

**2-16-2h** Illegal substitution and illegal participation fouls by R occurring at the snap (MechaniGram A) are enforced from the previous spot. Illegal participation fouls by team R occurring during the kick (MechaniGram B) are enforced under post-scrimmage kick enforcement.

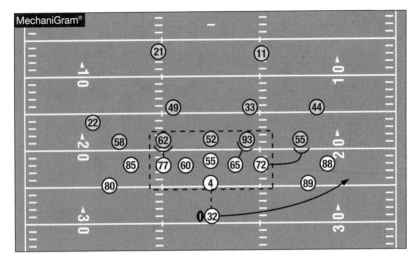

**2-17-1, 2-17-2, 2-17-4** It is legal for offensive linemen to block below the waist in the free-blocking zone, provided both players were on their lines of scrimmage and within the zone at the time of the snap and the block is an immediate, initial action following the snap. No. 77 could only block No. 62 below the waist if the block was immediate, initial action following the snap. No. 65 can block No. 93 below the waist even though No. 93 is playing off his shoulder, if the block is an immediate, initial action following the snap. No. 72 could not block No. 55 below the waist at any time during this play.

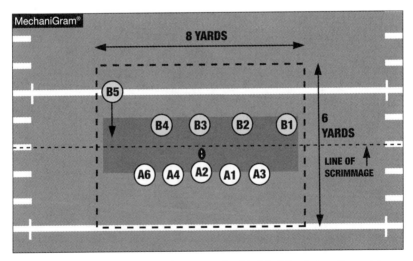

**2-17-2** In 11-player football, all players involved in blocking below the waist must be on the line of scrimmage and in the free-blocking zone at snap. Also, the contact must take place in the zone. B5 moves to line of scrimmage just prior to the ball being snapped and therefore meets the definition of a lineman.

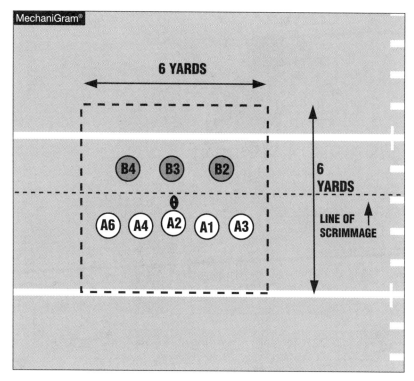

**6 YARDS**

B4  B3  B2

A6  A4  A2  A1  A3

6 YARDS

LINE OF SCRIMMAGE

**2-17-2** In nine- eight- and six-player football, the free-blocking zone is a square area extending laterally 3 yards either side of the spot of the snap and 3 yards behind each line of scrimmage.

PlayPic®

A

**FREE-BLOCKING ZONE**

PlayPic®

B

**FREE-BLOCKING ZONE**

**2-17-2c** In PlayPic A, both players are in the free-blocking zone and on their lines of scrimmage. In PlayPic B, the block is legal because it is in the zone at the time of the snap, is an immediate, initial action following the snap, and both players began the play on their lines of scrimmage and in the free-blocking zone.

**2-18** A fumble (PlayPic A) is any loss of player possession other than by kick, pass or handing. A fumble may be recovered and advanced by any player of either team. A muff (PlayPic B) occurs when a player touches a loose ball in an unsuccessful attempt to gain possession.

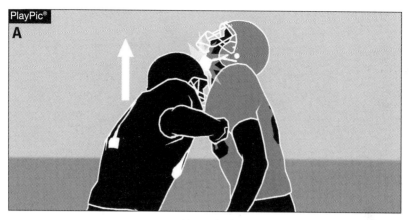

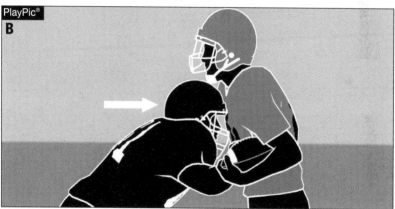

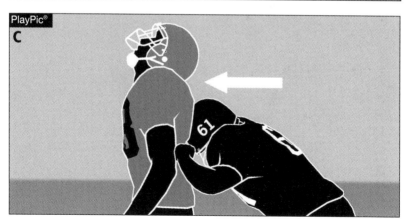

**2-20; 9-4-3i; 9-4-3i Note** Illegal helmet contact is dangerous. Butt blocking (PlayPic A), face tackling (PlayPic B) and spearing (PlayPic C) are all fouls carrying a 15-yard penalty.

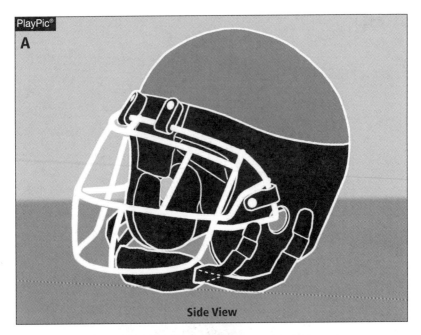

**Side View**

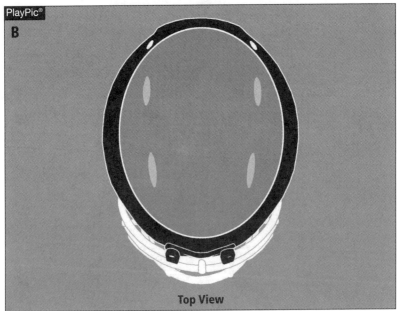

**Top View**

**2-20-1c** Spearing is an act by any player who initiates contact against an opponent at the shoulders or below with the crown (top portion) of their helmet. The shaded area is the crown.

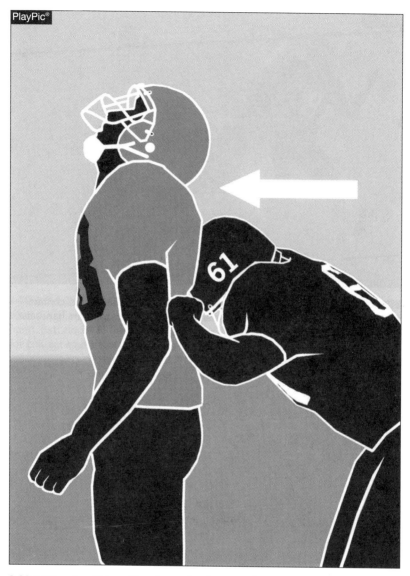

**2-20-1c** Number 61 is guilty of spearing because the crown (top portion) of their helmet was used to initiate contact against an opponent at the shoulders or below.

**2-20-2; 9-4-3m** Targeting is an act by any player who takes aim and initiates contact against an opponent above the shoulders with the helmet, forearm, hand, fist to the head (PlayPic) elbow or shoulders. Targeting may be called for contact against any opponent, including the runner.

**2-20-2, 9-4-3m** A blow to the helmet by two linemen in the free blocking zone is not necessarily a targeting foul.

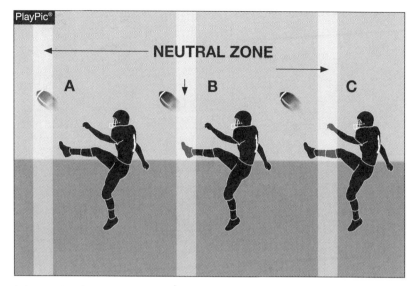

**NEUTRAL ZONE**

A  B  C

**2-24-4** A legal scrimmage kick is made from in or behind the neutral zone as in PlayPics A and B. As in a forward-pass play, the down marker can be used as a reference point because it denotes the forward limit of the neutral zone. In PlayPic C it is an illegal kick because the kicker's foot was beyond the neutral-zone plane on contact.

**2-24-9** When the ball is illegally kicked, the ball retains its original status. The player in PlayPic A fumbles and the player in PlayPic B kicks the loose ball. The ball remains a fumble.

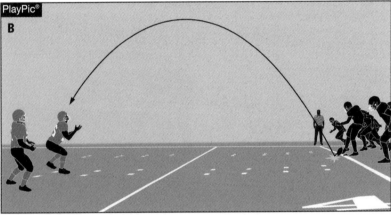

**2-24-10; 6-1-11; 6-1 PENALTY** A pop-up kick is a free kick in which the kicker drives the ball immediately to the ground, the ball strikes the ground once and goes into the air in the manner of a ball kicked directly off the tee. Such kicks will be penalized as a dead-ball foul.

**2-25-2** Only one player may not be on the line but still penetrate the vertical plane through the waistline of his nearest teammate who is on the line. This player (A) must be in position to receive a hand-to-hand snap, but does not have to actually receive it. By rule, he is the only player allowed to be positioned in "no man's land" at the snap. All other players not on the line must be clearly positioned as backs. The player marked (B) is in an illegal position.

B's END ZONE

**2-26-3** A touchdown is scored even though the ball has not penetrated the goal-line plane inside the sideline since the runner is touching inbounds when the ball breaks the plane of the goal-line extended, it is a touchdown. However, if the runner is not touching inbounds when the ball breaks the plane of the goal-line extended, it is not a touchdown and the ball is spotted where it broke the sideline plane.

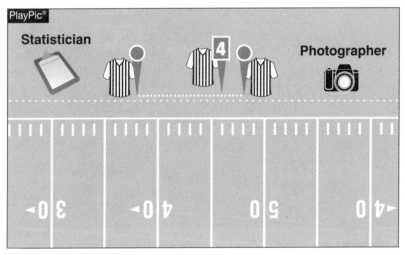

Statistician

4

Photographer

**2-26-8; 9-8-3** A restraining line is a line placed around the outside of the field. No person, including but not limited to, spectators, game administrators or members of the media, shall be allowed within the restraining line. A maximum of three coaches as well as permitted nonplayers are allowed within the restraining line in front of the team box, as provided for in Rule 9-8-3, as long as the ball is dead.

**2-31-2 Note** The game official must rule whether the action illustrated results in a fumble or an incomplete pass. The game official is to make his judgement based upon the movement of the passer's arm at contact. If the arm is stationary or moving backward away from the line of scrimmage on contact (PlayPic A), the result is a fumble. If the arm is moving forward toward the line of scrimmage on contact (PlayPic B), the result is an incomplete pass.

**K MISSES BALL**
**R MAKES CONTACT**

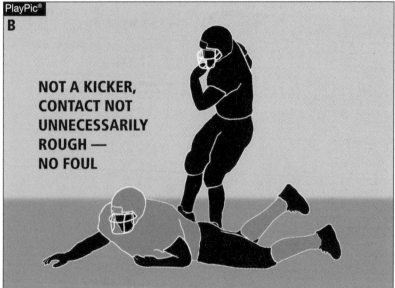

**NOT A KICKER,**
**CONTACT NOT**
**UNNECESSARILY**
**ROUGH —**
**NO FOUL**

**2-32-8** A player becomes a kicker when his knee, lower leg or foot makes contact with the ball. When the player in PlayPic A "whiffs" on the kick, he is not considered a kicker. The contact by the opponent only caused the K player to lose his balance and was not unnecessarily rough (PlayPic B). There is no foul.

**KICKER STARTS TO RUN**

**KICKER STOPS AND KICKS; R MAKES CONTACT**

**2-32-8** A player becomes a kicker when his knee, lower leg or foot makes contact with the ball. In PlayPic A, the K player is a runner, not a kicker. It is the defensive player's obligation by rule to avoid illegal contact. The covering official must judge if the defender had a reasonable opportunity to determine that a kick would be made.

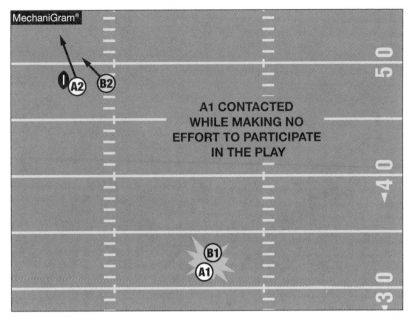

A1 CONTACTED
WHILE MAKING NO
EFFORT TO PARTICIPATE
IN THE PLAY

**2-32-16, 9-4-3i(3)** A defenseless player is a player who, because of his physical position and focus of concentration, is especially vulnerable to injury.

**2-32-16** After a kick (PlayPic A), a kicker who has not had a reasonable amount of time to regain his balance after the kick (PlayPic B) is a defenseless player.

**2-32-16** A pass receiver attempting to catch a pass, or a pass receiver who has clearly relaxed when the player has missed the pass or feels he can no longer catch the pass, is considered defenseless.

**2-32-16** A kick receiver attempting to catch or recover the ball is considered defenseless.

**2-32-16a** The player in PlayPic A is, by definition, a runner and is not defenseless. Once the ball is thrown, he is a passer and is defined as a defenseless player (PlayPic B).

**2-35, 3-6-1, 3-6-2a, 7-2-1** The referee gives a ready-for-play signal and the 25-second play clock begins before a try following a score; to start a period or overtime series; following administration of an inadvertent whistle; following a charged time-out and following an officials time-out.

**2-35, 3-6-1, 3-6-2a, 7-2-1** The play clock is set to 40 and is started immediately when a running play ends, team A gains a first down or after an incomplete pass.

PLAY CLOCK

**2-35, 3-6-1, 3-6-2a, 7-2-1** The runner goes out of bounds (PlayPic A). The play clock is set to 40 and is started immediately (PlayPic B). The ball is marked ready for play when the umpire sets the ball and walks away to his position (PlayPic C).

**2-35, 3-6-1, 3-6-2a, 7-2-1** When the 40-second play clock is in force, the ball is considered ready for play when the ball is placed and the umpire has moved to his position.

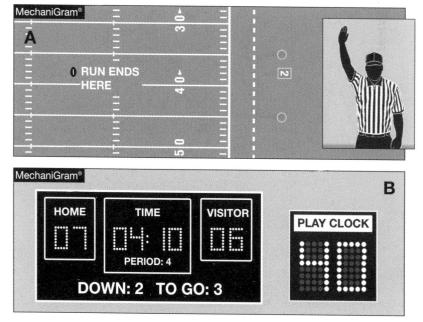

**2-35, 3-6-1, 3-6-2a, 7-2-1** When the covering official declares the ball dead with an upraised arm, the play clock begins its countdown from 40 seconds.

**2-39** It is a shift when the quarterback goes from his position in PlayPic A to his presnap position in PlayPic B. The movement of his head and/or shoulders in PlayPic B is not a shift, but would be a false start if it simulated the start of a play. After assuming the position in PlayPic B, the quarterback and the other players of A must be simultaneously stationary for at least one second before the snap or before a player goes in motion.

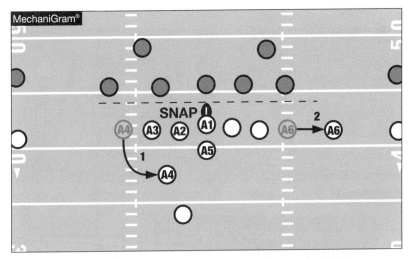

**2-39** Whether the movement in (1) and (2) is simultaneous or is done individually, it is a shift. It is a shift whether the movement is to the line, from the line or along the line. The movement of one or more A players to a new position is a shift. It is also a shift when the offensive team moves from the huddle or a player(s) goes from an upright or hands-on-knees position to a down position. Following a shift, all Team A players must be simultaneously set for at least one second before the snap or before a player goes in motion.

**2-45, 9-4-3o, 9-4-3o PENALTY** Tripping an opponent is a foul that carries a 15-yard penalty. Tripping is intentionally using the lower leg or foot to obstruct an opponent below the knees.

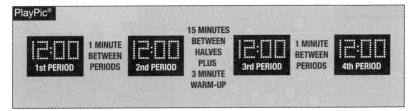

| | 1 MINUTE BETWEEN PERIODS | | 15 MINUTES BETWEEN HALVES PLUS 3 MINUTE WARM-UP | | 1 MINUTE BETWEEN PERIODS | |
|---|---|---|---|---|---|---|
| 12:00 1st PERIOD | | 12:00 2nd PERIOD | | 12:00 3rd PERIOD | | 12:00 4th PERIOD |

**TABLE 3-1** The normal 15-minute period between halves may be extended by state association approval to a maximum of 20 minutes upon proper notification at least five minutes prior to scheduled kickoff. By mutual agreement of the coaches, the halftime intermission may be reduced to a minimum of 10 minutes.

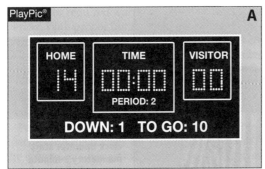

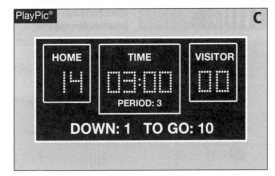

**TABLE 3-1** Immediately after the halftime intermission expires (PlayPic A), the referee must signal the timer (PlayPic B) to put 3 minutes on the game clock (PlayPic C) and to immediately start the game clock for the mandatory warm-up period. The head coach is responsible for his team being on the field for the mandatory warm-up at the end of the halftime intermission.

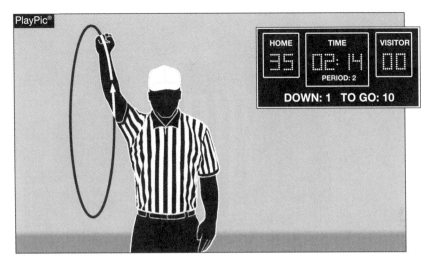

HOME
**35**

TIME
**02:14**
PERIOD: 2

VISITOR
**00**

DOWN: 1   TO GO: 10

**3-1-2; Table 1-7 (10)** State associations have the option to use the running game clock at any time during the game.

**3-1-5** When weather conditions are determined to be hazardous to the participants, the crew of game officials is authorized to delay the start or suspend the game. Interrupted games shall be continued from the point of interruption, unless the teams agree to accept the existing score as final, or there are conference, league or state association rules which apply.

**3-1-6c EXCEPTION** If weather causes a delay during the last three minutes of the second period, the opposing coaches may mutually agree to shorten the halftime intermission below the 10-minute minimum (PlayPic A). The mandatory 3-minute warm-up must take place before the third period begins (PlayPic B).

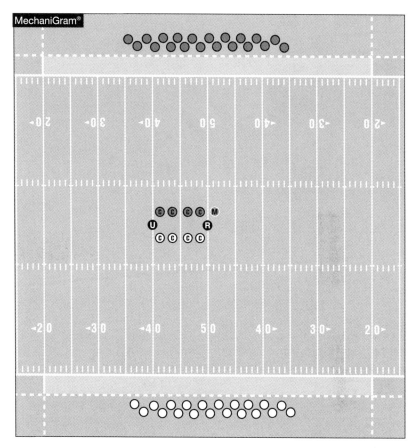

**3-2-2** When the coin toss or simulated coin toss occurs three minutes before game time, not more than four team members in game uniform (captains) from each team shall be present for the coin toss. Others present at the coin toss are game management decisions in compliance with state association policy. All other team members in game uniform must remain outside the field of play.

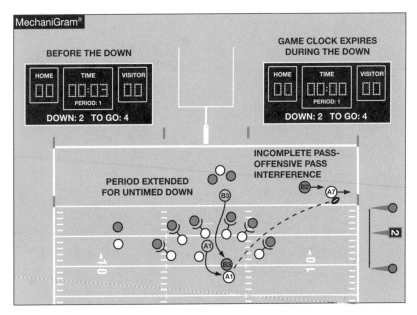

**3-3-3, 3-3-4** Team A commits a live-ball foul and time for the period expires during the down. As shown in the MechaniGram, if the penalty is accepted, the period is extended for an untimed down.

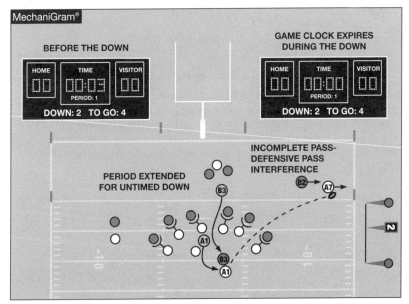

**3-3-3, 3-3-4** Team B commits a live-ball foul and time for the period expires during the down. As shown in the MechaniGram, if the penalty is accepted, the period is extended for an untimed down.

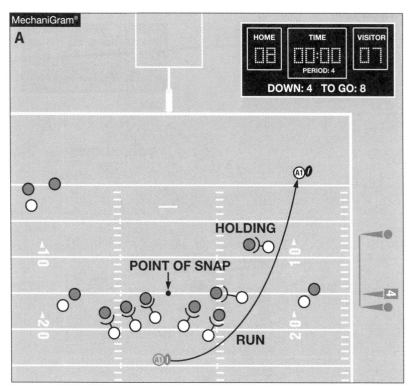

**A**

HOME | TIME | VISITOR
08 | 00:00 | 07
PERIOD: 4

DOWN: 4 TO GO: 8

A1

HOLDING

POINT OF SNAP

RUN

A1

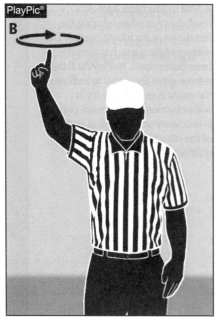

PlayPic®

**B**

**3-3-3a** Since the offensive holding foul in MechaniGram A occurred during the last timed down of a period, the period will be extended with an untimed down if the penalty is accepted. If the penalty is declined, the touchdown is scored and the period is over following the try. An unsportsmanlike foul or a nonplayer foul is not considered when determining if a period is to be extended because such penalty is automatically enforced from the succeeding spot. An untimed down is indicated by using the signal in PlayPic B.

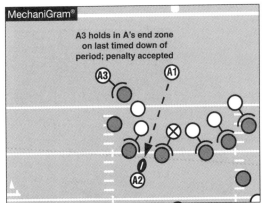

**MechaniGram®**

A3 holds in A's end zone on last timed down of period; penalty accepted

**PlayPic®**

| HOME | TIME | VISITOR |
|------|------|---------|
| 06 | 00:00 | 06 |
| | PERIOD: 4 | |

**DOWN: 1    TO GO: 10**

**PlayPic®**

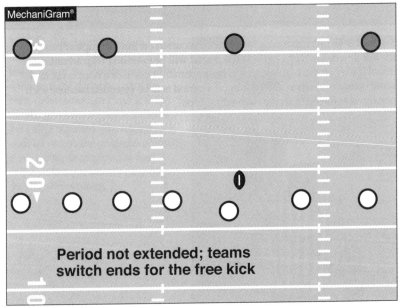

**MechaniGram®**

**Period not extended; teams switch ends for the free kick**

**3-3-4b(5)** If on the last timed down of a period enforcement of an accepted penalty results in a safety, the period is not extended for the ensuing free kick. The teams change goals and the free kick is the first play of the next period.

**3-3-6** This foul by B is a dead-ball foul. All dead-ball fouls after the end of the first half are enforced on the third period kickoff. If a dead-ball foul occurs after time has expired for any period, the penalty is measured from the succeeding spot. This succeeding spot could be the subsequent kickoff or the start of an overtime period.

**3-4-1a** During a kickoff or any other free kick (PlayPic A), the game clock will not be started until the ball is touched, other than first touching by. K. When K touches the ball beyond the neutral zone, as in PlayPic B, the game clock is started (PlayPic C). When K secures possession, the ball becomes dead and the game clock is stopped. K may not advance the ball. The recovery by K results in a first down for K.

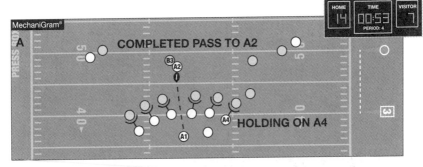

A

COMPLETED PASS TO A2

HOLDING ON A4

| HOME | TIME | VISITOR |
|------|------|---------|
| 14 | 00:53 | 7 |
| | PERIOD: 4 | |

B

C

**3-4-7** When a foul is committed with less than two minutes remaining in either half, the offended team has the option to start the game clock on the snap. In MechaniGram A, Team B trails when Team A fouls. Team B's coach is consulted (PlayPic B), choosing to decline the penalty and have the clock started on the snap (PlayPic C).

**3-5-1** Each team is entitled to three charged team time-outs during each half. Unused first half time-outs cannot be used in the second half. Unused second half time-outs cannot be used in overtime. The visiting team had all three charged team time-outs remaining in the second half and the home team had none (PlayPic A). Each team is entitled to one charged team time-out in each overtime period (PlayPic B).

**3-5-2a** The head coach or the head coach's designee may request a time-out.

**"ANOTHER TIME-OUT"**

**3-5-4** Successive charged time-outs may be granted each team during a dead-ball period provided the team has time-outs remaining. Each team is entitled to three during each half. Unused time-outs from the first half cannot be used in the second half or in overtime. No single charged time-out shall exceed one minute. When a team has used its allowable time-outs in each half, its coach and captain should be notified. A time-out may not be shortened unless both teams are ready to play.

**3-5-10a, 9-6-4b** It is an officials' time-out whenever a request is made for a designated injured player who is then required to leave the field for at least one down. The player must leave the game for one down, even if his team subsequently takes a charged time-out in this situation. It is illegal participation if the injured player does not stay out for at least one down unless the halftime intermission or an overtime intermission occurs prior to the next down.

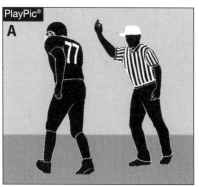

**3-5-10b** Any player who exhibits signs, symptoms or behaviors consistent with a concussion (such as loss of consciousness, headache, dizziness, confusion or balance problems) shall be immediately removed from the game (PlayPic A) and shall not return to play until cleared by an appropriate health-care professional (PlayPic B).

**3-5-10c** When a game official discovers any player who is bleeding, has an open wound, has any amount of blood on his/her uniform, or has blood on his/her person, he shall stop the game clock or delay the ready-for-play signal. The player must leave the game for at least one down under provisions of the apparently injured-player rule. The bleeding must be stopped, the wound covered, the uniform and/or body appropriately cleaned and/or the uniform changed before returning to competition.

**3-5-10d** If any player's helmet comes completely off during the down, or subsequent dead-ball action related to the down, and it is not due to a foul by the opponent (PlayPic A), that player must leave the game for at least one down unless the halftime intermission or an overtime intermission occurs (PlayPic B). In such circumstances, an officials' time-out occurs. Note that if the player whose helmet comes completely off has possession of the ball, the ball is dead immediately.

**3-5-10d** If a player's helmet comes completely off during the down and it is directly attributable to a foul by an opponent (PlayPic A), the penalty is enforced but the player need not leave the game (PlayPic B).

PlayPic®

PLAY CLOCK
40

NEUTRAL ZONE →

**3-6-1a(1)e EXCEPTION 2** When the clock is stopped due to Rule 3-5-7i and Team B is the only team to foul, the play clock will be set to 40 seconds.

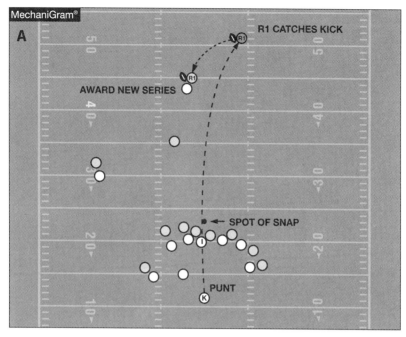

MechaniGram®

A

R1 CATCHES KICK

AWARD NEW SERIES

SPOT OF SNAP

PUNT

PlayPic®

B

PLAY CLOCK
25

**3-6-1a(1)f** When Team R is awarded a new series after a legal kick (MechaniGram A), the play clock is set to 25 seconds and starts with the ready-for-play signal (PlayPic B).

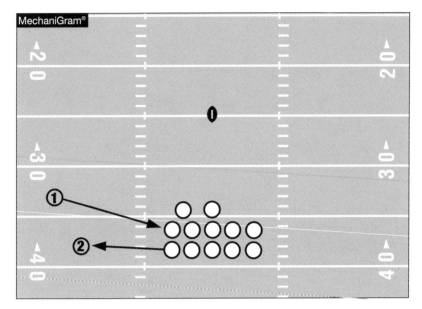

**3-7-1** A replaced player must begin to leave the field within three seconds. The three seconds begins when a player becomes a replaced player as defined in 2-32-12 and a substitute becomes a player as defined in 2-32-15. It is not a foul to break a huddle with more than 11 players as long as the replaced player begins to leave the field within three seconds.

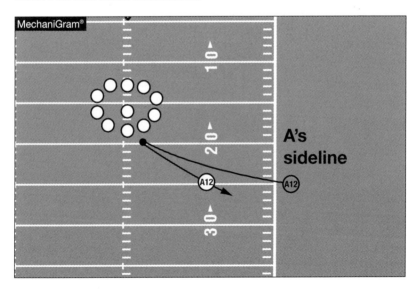

**3-7-2** A player, replaced player or a substitute who is unable to complete the substitution is required to leave the field at the side on which his team box is located.

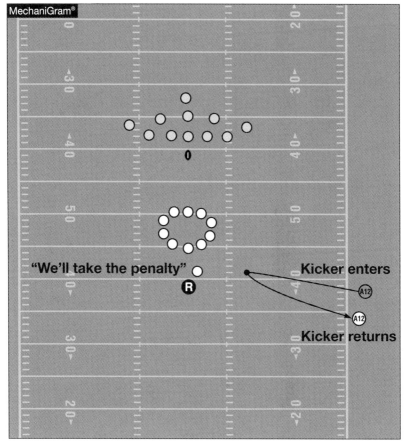

MechaniGram®

"We'll take the penalty"

Kicker enters

A12

A12

Kicker returns

**3-7-3** Following a third-down play, a substitute for Team A enters the field for an apparent punting situation. However, a foul has occurred during the down and Team A accepts the penalty. The substitute who previously entered is allowed to return to his team box since the penalty acceptance cancels the unwanted substitution.

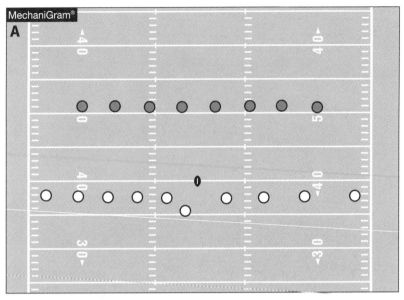

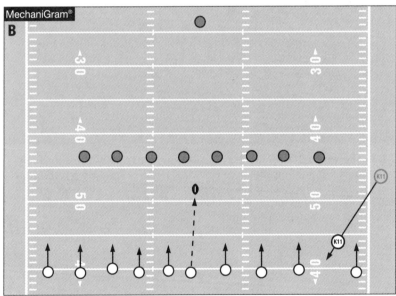

**3-7-5** In MechaniGram A, K has 10 players on the field. Although K11 is in the neutral zone after the ball has been declared ready (MechaniGram B), it is not encroachment. An entering substitute is not a player for encroachment purposes until he reaches his team's side of the neutral zone. Since the ball is kicked with K11 in the neutral zone, the ball is live and it is an illegal-substitution foul for not being on his team's side of the neutral zone when the ball is kicked.

# Part 3
## Rule 4

## Ball in Play, Dead Ball and Out of Bounds

There are two ways to put the ball in play, with a free kick or with a snap. The ball remains dead and a down is not begun if a snap or free kick is attempted before the ball is ready for play, or there is an illegal snap or other snap infraction. Each half is started with a kickoff. A kickoff also puts the ball in play after a successful field goal and following a try. A free kick follows a safety and if chosen, following a fair catch or awarded catch.

The ball becomes dead and the down is ended:

1. When a runner goes out of bounds or his forward progress is stopped.
2. When a live ball goes out of bounds.
3. When a forward pass (legal or illegal) is incomplete.
4. When a legal kick breaks the plane of R's goal line, unless a field goal is scored.
5. When a loose ball is on the ground and no player attempts to secure possession.
6. When a loose ball is simultaneously caught or recovered by opposing players.
7. When a loose ball is touched by or touches anything inbounds other than a player, substitute, game official, the ground, etc.
8. When the kickers catch or recover any free kick.
9. When the kickers catch or recover a scrimmage kick beyond the neutral zone.
10. When prior to any touching by R, the kickers touch a scrimmage kick beyond the neutral zone after it has come to rest.
11. Following a valid or invalid fair-catch signal when the kick is caught or recovered by R.
12. When a touchdown or field goal is scored.
13. During a try when B secures possession or it is apparent the kick will not score.
14. When the helmet comes completely off a player in possession of the ball.
15. Whenever a game official sounds a whistle inadvertently.

When the ball goes out of bounds, the out-of-bounds spot is fixed by the yard line through the ball's foremost point. When a runner goes out of bounds, the inbounds spot is fixed by the yard line through the foremost point of the ball at the time the runner crosses the plane of the sideline.

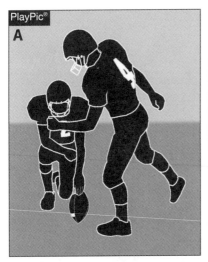

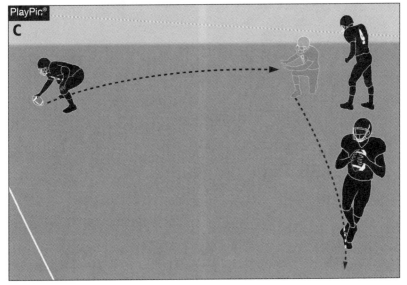

**4-2-2a EXCEPTION** No. 4 is in position to kick and the holder has a knee(s) on the ground at the snap in PlayPic A. The exception to the basic dead-ball rule is in effect when both these conditions are being met at the snap. The ball remains live for a kick as in PlayPic B, or if the holder rises with the ball (PlayPic C) to run, pass or drop kick.

**4-2-2a EXCEPTION** A holder with his knee(s) on the ground who has a teammate in position to kick at the snap as in PlayPic A, is allowed to rise to catch or recover an errant snap. The ball remains live if he goes to his knee(s) immediately after catching or recovering the snap. The holder is then allowed in PlayPic C or PlayPic D to do what he could have done if the snap had been accurate and he had not risen from his knee(s) to begin with. If the snap is muffed or the holder fumbles, he may recover with his knee(s) on the ground and place the ball for a kick or he may rise with it.

## BACKWARD PASS

**4-2-2e** The backward pass is not caught in PlayPic A. When opposing players simultaneously possess a backward pass, as in PlayPic B, the ball becomes dead immediately. This ball belongs to the passing team.

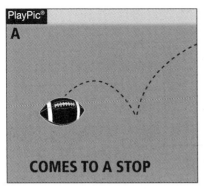

**4-2-2f** When a scrimmage kick rolls to a complete stop (PlayPic A) and it is touched by K (PlayPic B), the covering official will immediately sound his whistle to indicate the ball is dead. In PlayPic C the R player is advancing with a dead ball. Touching by K of a scrimmage kick at rest is not first touching.

**4-2-2l** The player has a prosthetic arm. If the prosthetic limb comes completely off the runner, the ball becomes dead and the down ends.

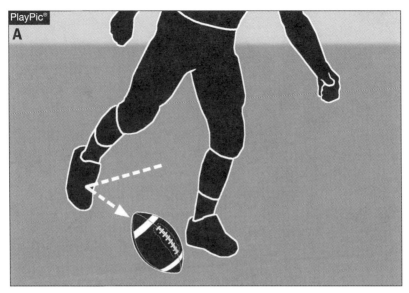

← LINE OF SCRIMMAGE

**4-2-3b** The inadvertent-whistle procedure is the same for action in PlayPics A, B and C. If the ball is loose and the whistle sounds following an illegal kick, fumble, illegal forward pass or backward pass, the team last in possession may take the results of the play where possession was lost or replay the down. In PlayPic A or PlayPic C, if the penalty is accepted, the administration of the foul takes precedence over the inadvertent whistle.

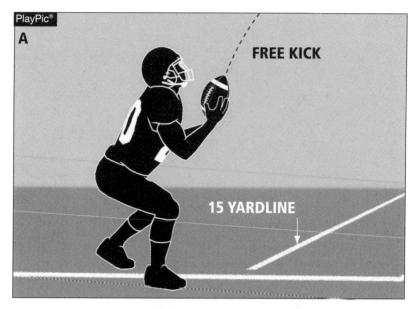

**PlayPic®**

**A**

FREE KICK

15 YARDLINE

**PlayPic®**

**B**

FREE KICK

15 YARDLINE

OUT OF BOUNDS

**4-3-1, 6-1-9** In PlayPic A, since the receiver possesses the free kick before he touched out of bounds with the ball inside the sideline plane, he is considered to have caused the ball to be out of bounds. The ball will be put in play at the inbounds spot on the 14-yard line. In PlayPic B, since there was no touching by R prior to the player being out of bounds, K has caused the free kick to go out of bounds R may either put the ball in play from the inbounds spot, put the ball in play 25 yards beyond the previous spot, or have the 5-yard penalty enforced against the kicking team enforced from the previous spot and kick off again, or have the 5-yard penalty enforced from the succeeding spot.

**RUNNER HIT BY TACKLER**

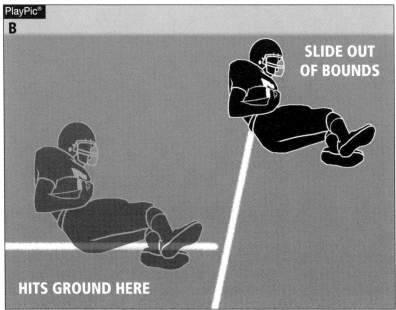

**SLIDE OUT OF BOUNDS**

**HITS GROUND HERE**

**4-2-2a** The runner is inbounds when he is hit by an opponent (PlayPic A). The ball is dead when the runner hits the ground (PlayPic B). Even though the runner slides out of bounds, the ball has not been out of bounds and the game clock continues to run. The ball is placed at its forward point where the ball became dead. The runner is down when any part of his person, other than hand or foot, touches the ground.

**4-3-3** A ball in player possession is out of bounds when the runner or the ball touches anything, other than another player or game official, which is on or outside the sideline or end line. The spot where the ball becomes dead is under the foremost point of the ball in possession of the runner when he crosses the plane of the sideline at B's one-yard line (PlayPic A). No touchdown is scored in PlayPic B since the runner was airborne and was not touching inbounds when the ball broke the plane of the goal-line extended.

# Part 3
Rule 5

## Series of Downs, Number of Downs and Team Possession After Penalty

The team which puts the ball in play by scrimmage after a free kick, touchback or fair catch, is awarded a series of four consecutively numbered downs in which to advance the ball to or beyond the line to gain. A new series is awarded if the ball belongs to the offensive team on or beyond the line to gain. It is also a new series and the ball will belong to the defensive team at the end of any down, if B gained possession during that down, or at the end of a fourth down, if the offensive team was in possession behind the line to gain. If a receiver is the first to touch a scrimmage kick while it is beyond the neutral zone, a new series will be awarded to the team in possession at the end of the down, unless the penalty is accepted for a non post-scrimmage kick foul which occurred before the kick ended.

When a penalty is declined, the number of the next down is the same as if the foul had not occurred. When a foul by A (or K) or B (or R) occurs during a scrimmage down and before any change of team possession, and before a receiver is first to touch a scrimmage kick while it is beyond the neutral zone, the ball belongs to A (or K) after penalty enforcement. The number of the next down is the same as that of the down during which the foul occurred unless acceptance of the penalty carries an automatic first down or loss of down, or the penalty enforcement or advance results in a first down. The loss of down aspect of a penalty has no significance following a change of possession or if the line to gain is reached after enforcement.

When a foul by A or B occurs prior to a scrimmage down, or simultaneously with the snap, the number of the next down after enforcement is the same as the number established before the foul occurred, unless enforcement for a foul by B results in a first down. After a distance penalty, the ball belongs to the team in possession at the time of the foul. Team possession may then change if a new series is awarded.

**5-1-1b** In PlayPic A the down should be second, but the down marker indicator shows third during the down. After the ball is dead, the down marker indicator shows fourth and the other game officials point out the error to the referee (PlayPic B). The referee has the authority to correct the number of the next down prior to the ball becoming live after a new series of downs is awarded and prior to the declaration of the end of any period (PlayPic C).

**A. R TOUCHES**

**B. R HOLDS**

**C. K RECOVERS**

**5-1-3f** The series is not ended if K accepts the penalty for the foul during a loose-ball play. In this play, K will undoubtedly take the results of the play, decline the penalty and take the ball at the spot of recovery as this is not a PSK foul, so acceptance would result in a replay.

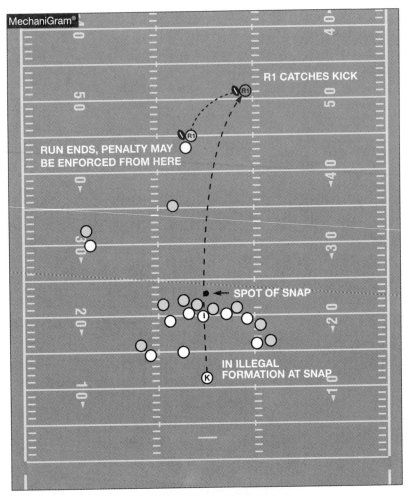

**MechaniGram®**

R1 CATCHES KICK

R1

RUN ENDS, PENALTY MAY
BE ENFORCED FROM HERE

SPOT OF SNAP

IN ILLEGAL
FORMATION AT SNAP

**5-2-2; 5-2-4; 10-4-2c EXCEPTION; 10-5-1j** Team R may choose penalty enforcement from the succeeding spot for a foul other than kick-catching interference that occurs from the start of a kick down until the legal kick ends.

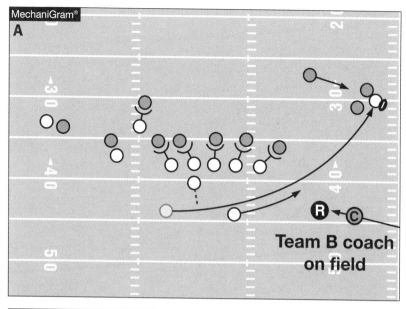

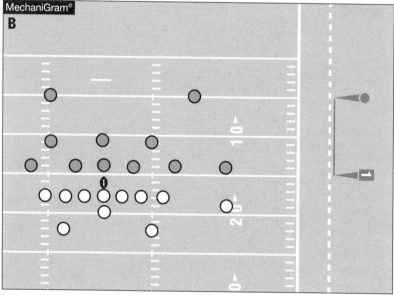

**5-3-1** When a new series is gained as in MechaniGram A, the penalty for the unsportsmanlike foul is administered before the line to gain is established. In MechaniGram B, the line-to-gain indicator and down marker indicator are then set, making it first and 10 for Team A.

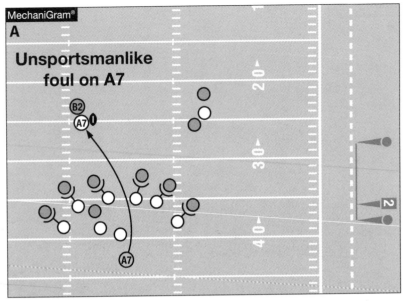

**A**

**Unsportsmanlike foul on A7**

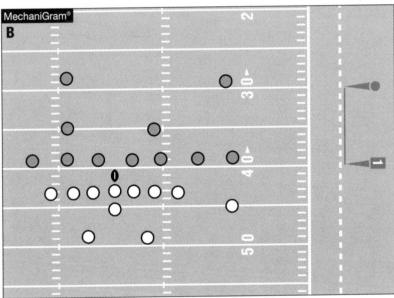

**B**

**5-3-1** Team A gains a first down, but A7 commits an unsportsmanlike foul after the down in MechaniGram A. Since the foul occurred prior to the subsequent ready-for-play, the line to gain is established following penalty enforcement. It is first and 10 for Team A in MechaniGram B.

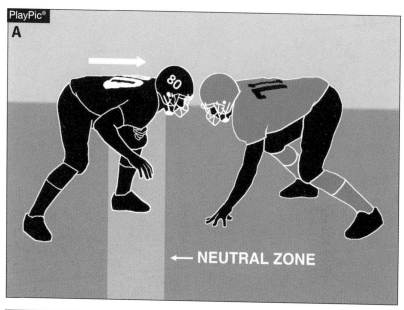

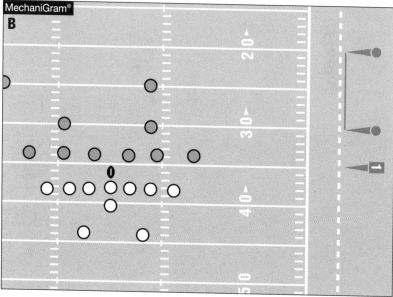

**5-3-1** Following the ready-for-play on first down, No. 80 encroaches (PlayPic A). It is first and 15 for Team A following penalty administration (MechaniGram B). A foul after the ready is the only situation where it will be more than first and 10 for Team A on the first snap of a new series.

**5-3-1** Team A is short of the line to gain on a fourth-down play after enforcement of all live-ball fouls, which dictates it is a new series for Team B. The penalty for the dead-ball illegal personal contact seen in PlayPic A is enforced before the chain and box are set for B's series. It is first and 10 for Team B at B's 35-yard line (PlayPic B).

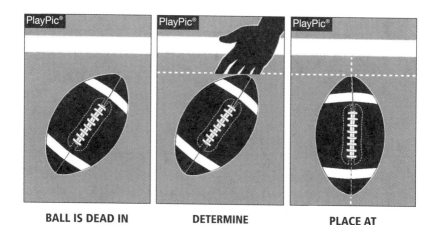

**BALL IS DEAD IN THIS POSITION**  **DETERMINE FORWARD POINT**  **PLACE AT FORWARD POINT**

**5-3-2** Whenever a measurement is required, the ball shall be placed with its long axis parallel with the sideline before measurement. If it is a first down, the referee gives the signal, spots it and marks it ready for play. If the line to gain has not been reached, the referee signals the distance needed to both sides.

# Part 3
## Rule 6

## Kicking the Ball and Fair Catch

A free kick is used to put the ball in play to start a free-kick down. A free-kick line is established for each team and is always 10 yards apart. If not moved because of a penalty, K's free-kick line for a kickoff is its 40-yard line, its 20-yard line for a kick following a safety, and the yard line through the spot of the catch following a fair catch.

The offensive team may punt, drop kick or placekick from in or behind the neutral zone before team possession has changed Such a kick is a scrimmage kick. When any member of the kicking team touches a scrimmage kick between the goal lines and beyond the neutral zone, before it is touched by a member of the receiving team and before the ball has come to rest, it is first touching. First touching does not cause the ball to become dead.

Any receiver may signal for a fair catch while any kick is in flight. Any receiver who gives a valid or invalid fair-catch signal is prohibited from blocking until the kick has ended.

If any receiver gives a valid signal for a fair catch and he catches the free kick in or beyond the neutral zone and between the goal lines, or catches the scrimmage kick beyond the neutral zone and between the goal lines, it is a fair catch and the ball becomes dead. Only the receiver who gives a valid signal is afforded protection and only where a fair catch may be made. If, after a receiver gives a valid signal, the catch is made by a teammate, it is not a fair catch but the ball becomes dead. Following a valid or invalid signal by the receiving team, the ball becomes dead when caught or recovered by any receiver.

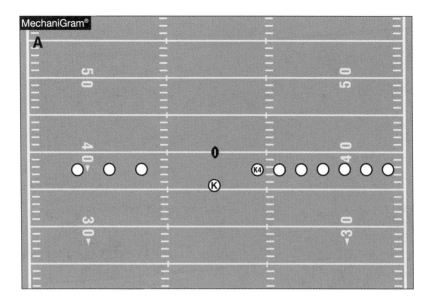

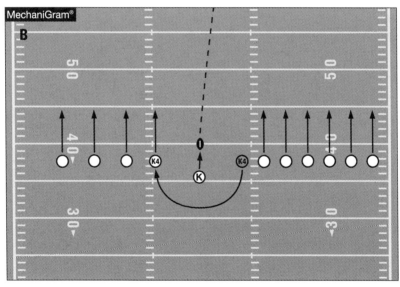

**6-1-3; 6-1-4; 6-1 PENALTY** In MechaniGram A, K has only three players on one side of the kicker. If K4 shifts to the other side of the kicker by going more than five yards from the free kick line after the ready-for-play (MechaniGram B), it is a dead-ball foul for free-kick infraction.

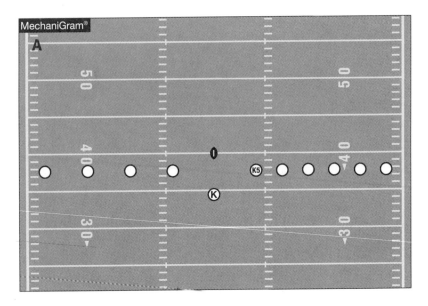

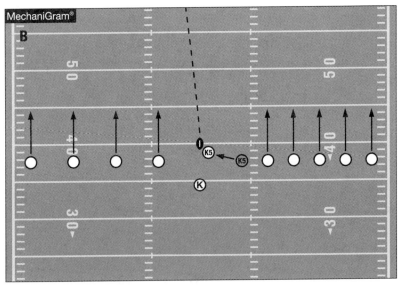

**6-1-3; 6-1-4; 6-1 PENALTY** The formation in MechaniGram A is legal. In MechaniGram B, K5 (who was not more than five yards behind his free-kick line) kicks the ball. That is a foul. When a player is more than five yards behind the kicking team's free-kick line, that player is the only player who may legally kick the ball.

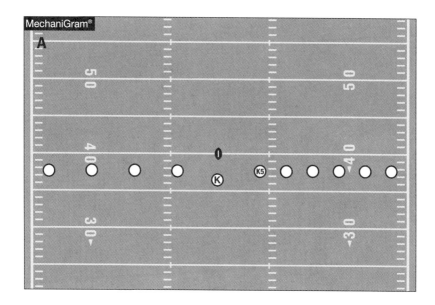

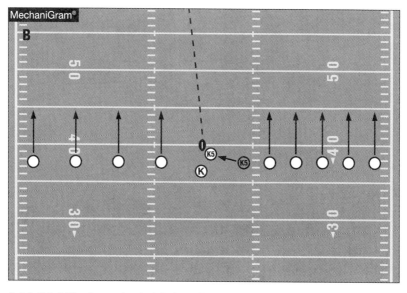

**6-1-3; 6-1-4** The formation in MechaniGram A is legal. In MechaniGram B, when K5 kicks the ball, there are still at least four players on either side of the kicker. There is no foul. K had no player more than five yards behind the kicking team's free-kick line and had four on either side of the kicker at the time of the kick.

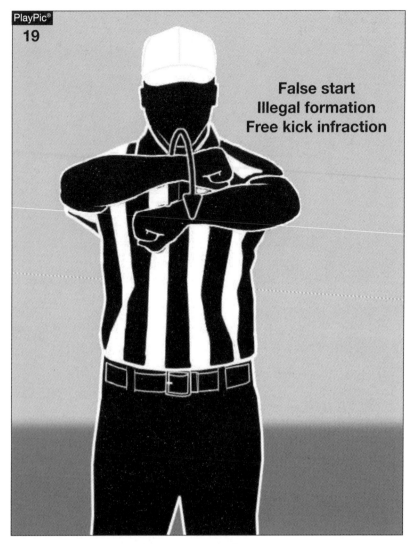

**False start
Illegal formation
Free kick infraction**

**6-1-3b PENALTY, 6-1-4 PENALTY** Signal 19 is used to indicate fouls for K player(s) more than 5 yards behind his free-kick line, a K player more than 5 yards behind his free-kick line and any other player kicking the ball, and K not having at least 4 players on each side of kicker at the time of the kick.

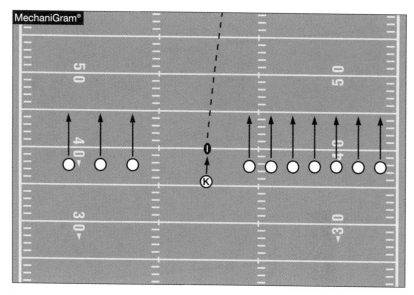

**6-1-4** At the time the ball is kicked, at least four K players must be on each side of the kicker. In the MechaniGram, K is guilty of a free-kick infraction, a dead-ball foul.

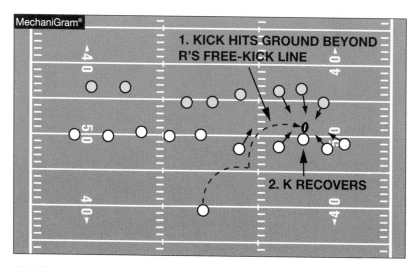

**1. KICK HITS GROUND BEYOND R'S FREE-KICK LINE**

**2. K RECOVERS**

**6-1-6** If the free kick has gone beyond the plane of the receiver's free-kick line and has touched the ground, any K player may then recover. Both conditions must be met — has touched the ground and has gone beyond the plane. The order of occurrence has no bearing on the fact that K may then recover K may not advance a recovered kick.

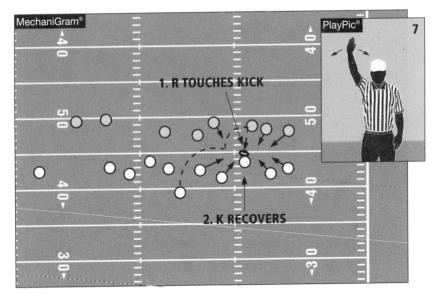

**1. R TOUCHES KICK**

**2. K RECOVERS**

**6-1-6** When the free kick is touched first by a receiver before it has gone 10 yards, it may be recovered by any K player. The recovery causes the ball to become dead and the down is ended. No K player may advance the recovered kick. However, it is a first down for K.

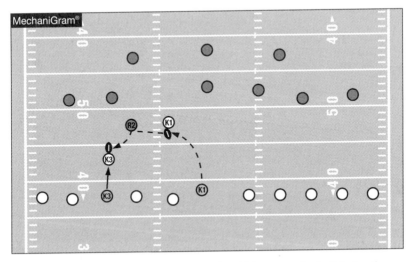

**6-1-6** K1's muff in the neutral zone on a free kick causes the ball to touch R2 and K3 recovers. Because R2's touching was caused by K1's muff, the touching by R2 is ignored as they will accept first touching by K1. It will be R's ball at the second spot of first touching.

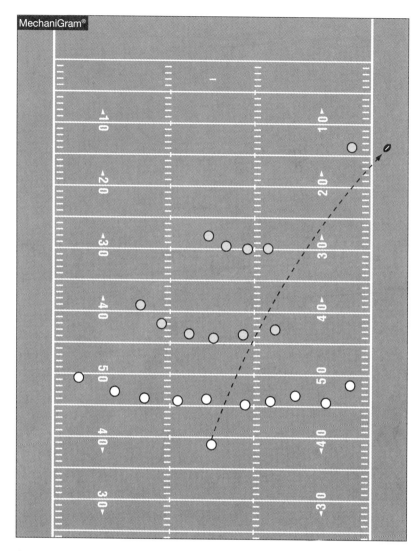

**6-1-9** It is a foul if a free kick untouched by R goes out of bounds between the goal lines. R may accept a 5-yard penalty from the previous spot and have K rekick; accept a 5-yard penalty from the succeeding spot; put the ball in play at the inbounds spot 25 yards beyond the previous spot; or decline the penalty and put the ball in play at the inbounds spot.

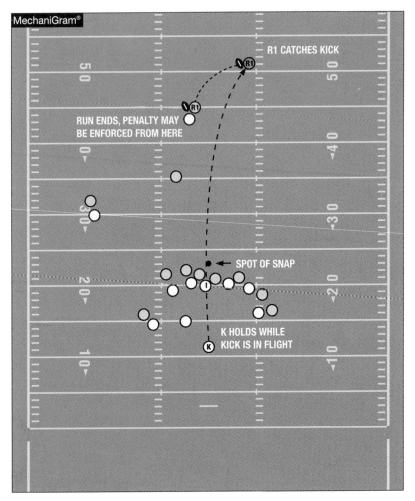

MechaniGram®

R1 CATCHES KICK

RUN ENDS, PENALTY MAY
BE ENFORCED FROM HERE

SPOT OF SNAP

K HOLDS WHILE
KICK IS IN FLIGHT

**6-1-9b, 6-1-9b PENALTY, 10-4-2 EXCEPTION, 10-5-1j** K fouls during a legal scrimmage kick and will not be next to put the ball in play. R may have the penalty enforced from the succeeding spot.

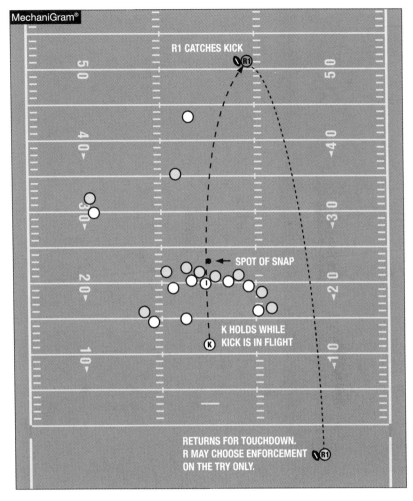

MechaniGram®

R1 CATCHES KICK

SPOT OF SNAP

K HOLDS WHILE
KICK IS IN FLIGHT

RETURNS FOR TOUCHDOWN.
R MAY CHOOSE ENFORCEMENT
ON THE TRY ONLY.

**6-1-9b, 6-1-9b PENALTY, 10-4-2 EXCEPTION, 10-5-1j** K fouls during a legal scrimmage kick, but R returns the kick for a touchdown. R may only have the penalty enforced on the try.

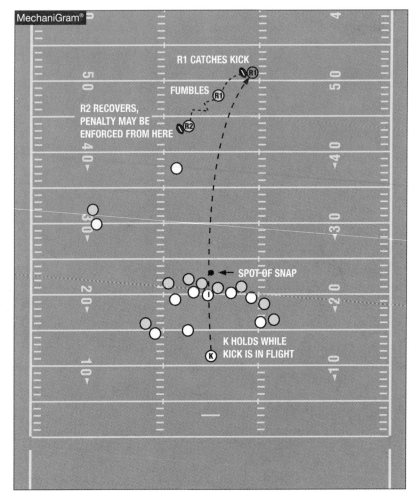

**6-1-9b, 6-1-9b PENALTY, 10-4-2 EXCEPTION, 10-5-1j** K fouls during a legal scrimmage kick. Despite the fumble, K will not be next to put the ball in play. R may have the penalty enforced from the succeeding spot.

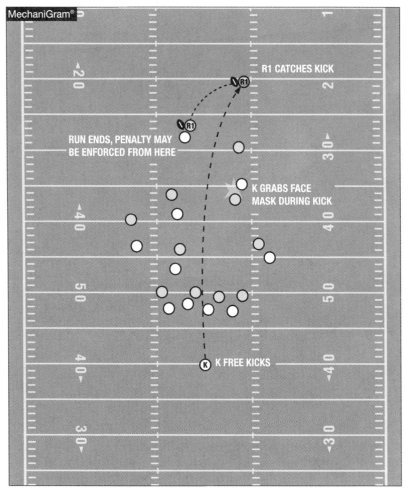

**6-1-9b, 6-1-9b PENALTY, 10-4-2 EXCEPTION, 10-5-1j** K fouls during a legal free kick and will not be next to put the ball in play. R may have the penalty enforced from the succeeding spot.

LINE OF SCRIMMAGE

← LINE OF SCRIMMAGE

**6-2-3** When a field-goal attempt fails, it is treated like any scrimmage kick and the ball remains live until the down ends. Since K recovered behind the neutral zone, they may advance. Game officials must be alert and not confuse a field-goal attempt with a try. When it is apparent there will be no score from a kick try, the down is ended.

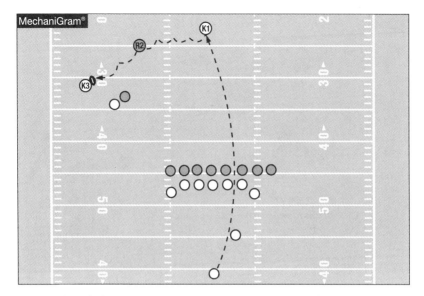

**6-2-4** K1 legally bats the scrimmage kick, which deflects off R2. The loose ball is recovered by K3. Because R2's touching was caused by K1's bat, the touching is ignored. R may take the ball at the spot of K3's recovery.

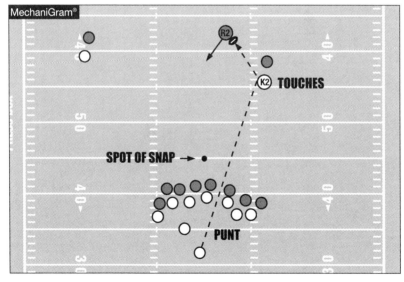

**6-2-5** First touching by the kicking team does not cause the ball to become dead. This is a legal advance. The right of R to take the ball at the spot of first touching by K is canceled if R touches the kick and thereafter commits a foul or if the penalty is accepted for any foul committed during the down.

**LINE OF SCRIMMAGE**

2 YARDS

**6-2-6** The neutral zone may be expanded up to a maximum of 2 yards behind the defensive line of scrimmage inside the boundary lines. No. 70 has touched a low scrimmage kick in the expanded neutral zone. The touching is ignored if the touching is in or behind the expanded neutral zone.

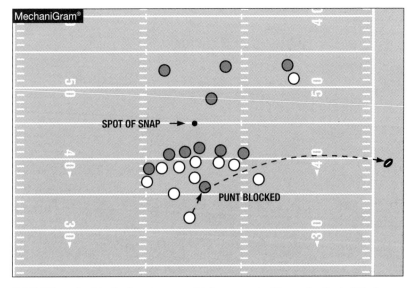

SPOT OF SNAP →

PUNT BLOCKED

**6-2-7** When the blocked scrimmage kick goes out of bounds, the ball belongs to the receiving team at the inbounds spot. This is true regardless of the down and distance when the scrimmage kick was made or where it went out of bounds between the goal line.

**6-3-1** When a potential scoring kick in flight is touched by R in his end zone, it does not become dead if the ball thereafter passes through the goal. The field goal counts. It would also count if the ball touched the crossbar or uprights and deflected through the goal. If R jumps up and blocks the kick away from the goalposts, it causes the ball to become dead immediately; and, on a field goal, it is a touchback.

**6-5-1** This is a legal block by K's No. 36 even though R's No. 80 may not advance if the kick is caught or recovered as a valid fair-catch signal was given. However, No. 80 may not block until the kick ends because he has signaled.

**6-5-6** Kick-catching interference. R has the option of taking the results of the play, accepting an awarded fair catch at the spot of the foul, accepting a 15-yard penalty from the spot of an awarded fair catch, or replaying the down after having the penalty enforced from the previous spot.

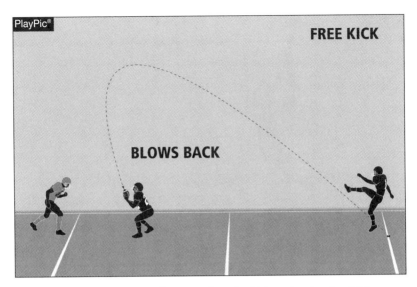

**6-5-6** It is kick-catching interference when the kickers touch a free kick in flight. It makes no difference whether or not the ball has been beyond the receiver's free-kick line. This restriction ends after a receiver touches the kick. R may choose an awarded fair catch at the spot of the foul with a 15-yard distance penalty or have the distance penalty enforced from the previous spot and rekick.

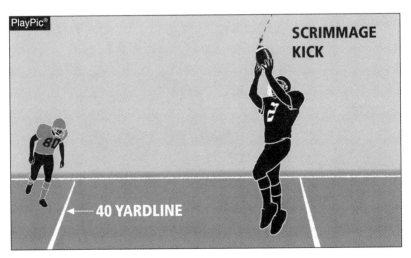

**6-5-6 EXCEPTION** A member of the kicking team legally catches a scrimmage kick beyond the neutral zone. This is only permissible when no member of the receiving team is in position to catch the ball. There is no requirement that the receiver must make or attempt to make a catch — only that he is in position where he could make a catch if he desired.

**6-5-6 EXCEPTION** Two R players are in position to attempt a catch. The opponent commits kick-catching interference. The receivers must be given an unobstructed opportunity to catch the kick. The ball becomes dead with the catch. R may accept an awarded fair catch at the spot of the foul, accept a 15-yard penalty from the spot of an awarded fair catch, or a replay of the down after having the penalty enforced from the previous spot.

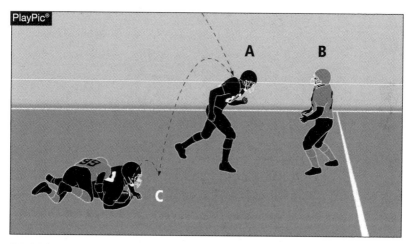

**6-5-6 EXCEPTION** The punt in flight hits another K player in the shoulder as he goes downfield to cover the kick (PlayPic A). A receiver is in position to make a catch (PlayPic B). It is kick-catching interference. R may accept an awarded fair catch following a 15-yard penalty from the spot of the foul or accept the penalty of 15 yards from the previous spot and a replay of the down. K's recovery (PlayPic C) is negated.

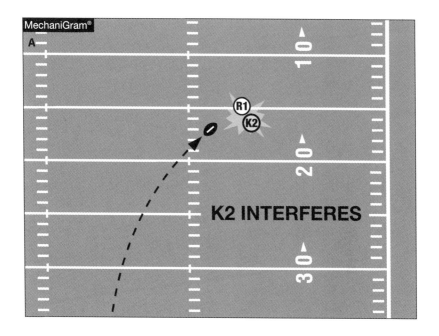

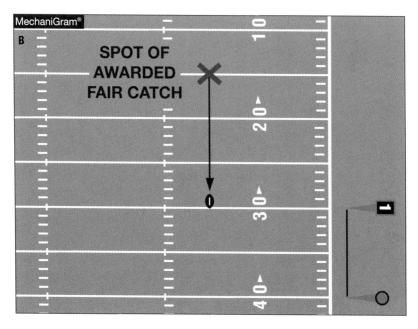

**6-5-6 PENALTY** K commits kick-catching interference (MechaniGram A). If R chooses an awarded fair catch, the 15-yard penalty may be enforced from the spot of the awarded fair catch (MechaniGram B).

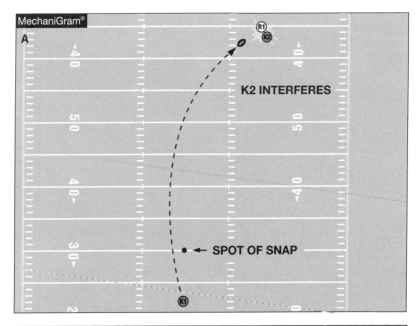

A

K2 INTERFERES

SPOT OF SNAP

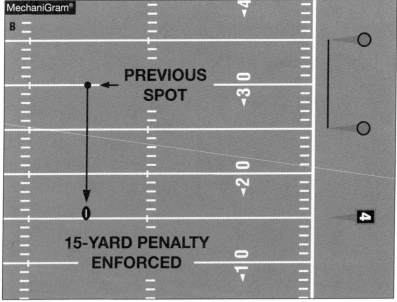

B

PREVIOUS
SPOT

15-YARD PENALTY
ENFORCED

**6-5-6 PENALTY** K commits kick-catching interference (MechaniGram A). R may choose enforcement of the 15-yard penalty from the previous spot and a replay of the down (MechaniGram B).

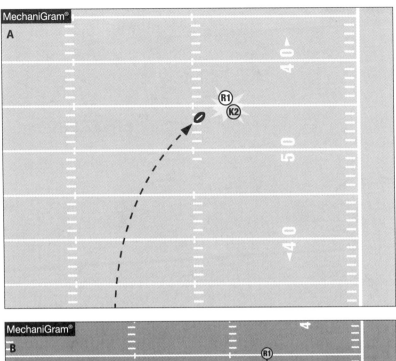

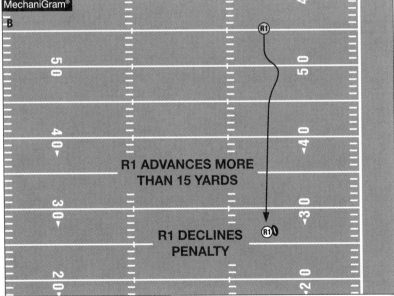

**6-5-6 PENALTY** K commits kick-catching interference (MechaniGram A). R may choose to decline the penalty and take the result of the play (MechaniGram B).

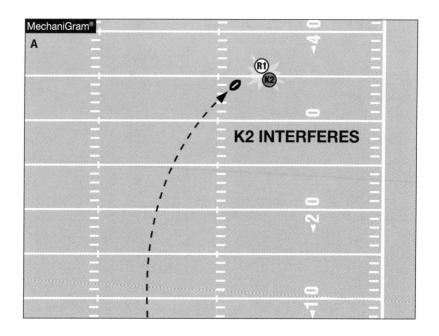

**MechaniGram®**

A

K2 INTERFERES

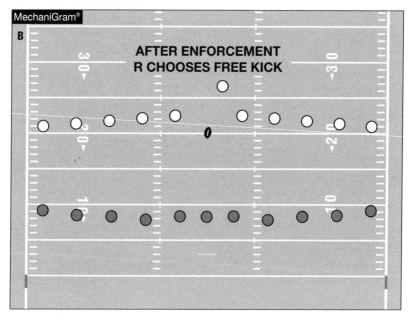

**MechaniGram®**

B

AFTER ENFORCEMENT
R CHOOSES FREE KICK

**6-5-4c, 6-5-6 PENALTY** K commits kick-catching interference (MechaniGram A). If R accepts the penalty for kick-catching interference, the 15-yard penalty may be enforced from the spot of the foul. R may then choose a free kick (MechaniGram B).

# Part 3
## Rule 7

## Snapping, Handling and Passing the Ball

For any scrimmage down, the ball may only become live with a legal snap. A snap is the legal act of passing or handing the ball from its position on the ground in a quick and continuous backward motion of the hand(s) during which the ball immediately leaves the hand(s). A snap ends when the ball touches the ground or a backfield player before it touches a Team A lineman.

The snap begins when the snapper first moves the ball other than in adjustment. The snapper is allowed to make certain preliminary adjustments while not changing the location of the ball. These preliminary movements may be made, but both hands may not be taken off the ball once the snapper has placed a hand(s) on the ball.

After the ball is ready and before the snap, each player of Team A must momentarily be within inside the 9-yard marks before the ball is snapped. Not more than one A player may be in motion at the snap and then only if such motion is not toward B's goal line. After a huddle or shift, all players of A must come to a stop and remain simultaneously stationary for at least one second before the snap.

A forward pass may be thrown only by the team which has put the ball in play from scrimmage, provided the ball is released with both feet of the passer in or behind the neutral zone. There may be only one legal forward pass during a down. During a pass, the ball travels in flight, that is, is thrown rather than handed forward.

During a forward pass, there are at least five ineligible receivers. On a pass which goes beyond the neutral zone, ineligibles may not go beyond the neutral zone before the pass is in flight. Ineligibles may go downfield if the pass does not go beyond the neutral zone. When a forward pass is touched by a defensive player, all A players become eligible immediately.

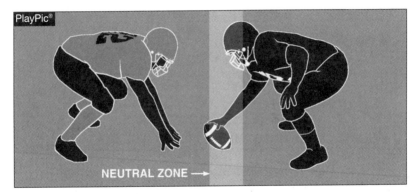

**7-1** A scrimmage down is started with a snap. The snapper's feet must be behind the neutral zone. His head may be in the neutral zone, but not beyond the foremost point of the ball. The ball may be preliminarily adjusted after which the snapper may not make a movement that simulates a snap. The snapper may not remove both hands once he has placed a hand(s) on the ball after the ready-for-play. The snap must be one continuous backward motion in which the ball immediately leaves the hand(s) of the snapper and must touch a Team A non-lineman or the ground before it touches a Team A lineman.

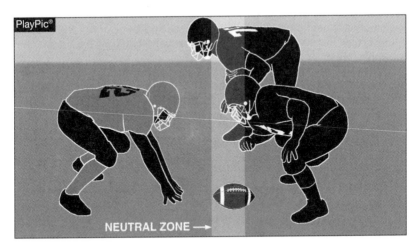

**7-1-6** Encroachment restrictions are not in effect for those in the neutral zone as the snapper has not placed a hand(s) on the ball. The players who are in the neutral zone may move and be out of the neutral zone before the snapper puts his hand(s), on the ball. Before the snapper places his hand(s) on the ball it is encroachment for any other player to touch the ball or an opponent or be in the zone to give defensive signals. All other encroachment restrictions begin after the ready-for-play when the snapper places his hand(s) on the ball.

NEUTRAL ZONE →

**7-1-6** After the ready for play and after the snapper is in contact with the ball, it is encroachment if a defensive player contacts the ball or the snapper's arms or hands until the snap is completed (Rule 2-40).

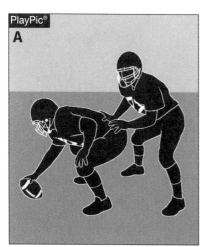 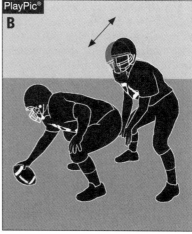

**7-1-7a** When the quarterback "chucks" his hands under the center (PlayPic A) or bobs his head (PlayPic B), it simulates snap action and is a false start. Jerky movements which simulate the beginning of the down or acts clearly intended to cause B to encroach are false starts. These acts must be judged on their own merits rather than whether or not B encroaches.

**7-1-9, 7-1-9 PENALTY** Disconcerting acts or words by the defense has been reclassified from an unsportsmanlike foul to a disconcerting act foul, and the penalty changed from 15 yards to 5 yards. Signal 23 will be used to indicate the foul.

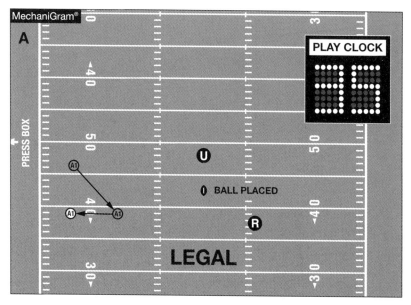

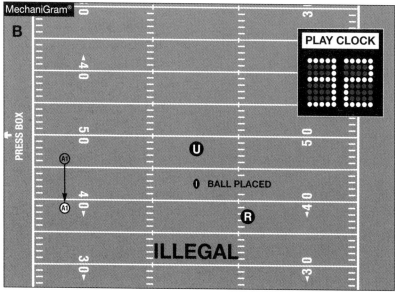

**7-2-1** In MechaniGram A, A1, who was downfield on the previous play, comes back inside the 9-yard marks prior to the umpire setting the ball with 35 seconds on the play clock and then immediately goes outside the marks after the ready-for-play. In MechaniGram B, A1 remains outside the 9-yard marks with 32 seconds on the play clock when the ball is placed by the umpire. The requirement remains in place that all players get inside the 9-yard marks after the ready-for-play and before the snap.

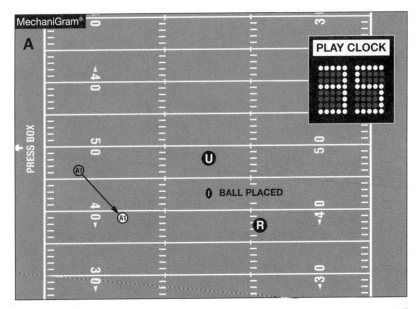

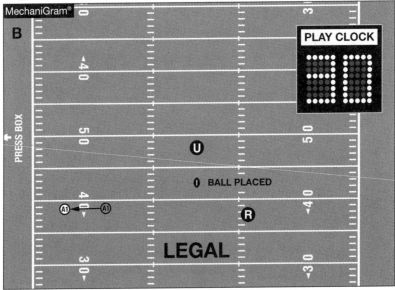

**7-2-1** In MechaniGram A, the ball is placed by the umpire with 35 seconds on the play clock and A1, who was downfield on the previous play, then comes back inside the 9-yard marks. In MechaniGram B, A1 then goes outside the 9-yard marks with 30 seconds on the play clock. That is legal. A1 has met the requirement to be inside the 9-yard marks after the ready-for-play and before the snap.

**7-2-3** If the ball is snapped, this would be an illegal formation foul at the snap. Of the A players who are not on their line at the snap, only one player may penetrate through the waistline of his nearest teammate who is on the line, and he must be in position to receive the snap, even though he is not required to receive it.

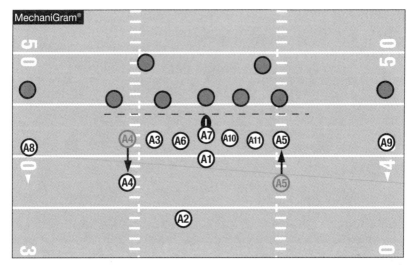

**7-2-6** The movement of one or more offensive players to new set positions is a shift. This formation is legal. A3 is now on the end of the line; if he is also wearing an eligible receiver's number, he is an eligible receiver. A9 is also on the end of the line and is eligible if he is wearing an eligible receiver's number. Following a shift, all players must simultaneously meet the one-second motionless requirement prior to the snap.

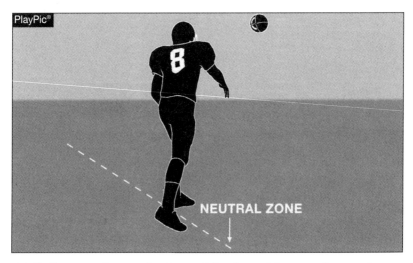

**7-5-2b** The passer has one foot beyond the plane of the neutral zone when he releases the ball on a forward pass. The pass is illegal. An illegal forward pass is part of a running play with the end of the run being the spot from which the pass is thrown.

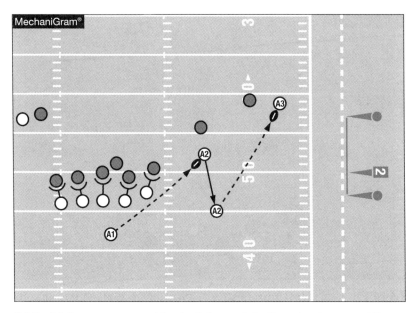

**7-5-2c** A1 throws a pass to A2, who is beyond the line of scrimmage. A2 retreats behind the line of scrimmage and then throws a pass to A3. The pass by A2 is an illegal pass as only one forward pass may be thrown.

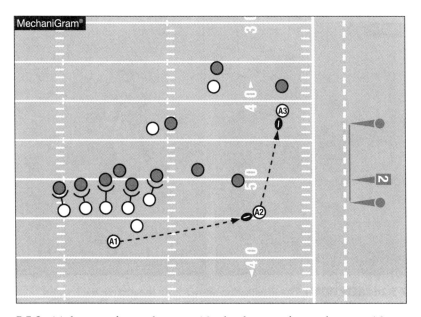

**7-5-2c** A1 throws a forward pass to A2 who throws a forward pass to A3. The pass by A2 is illegal. Only one forward pass may be thrown.

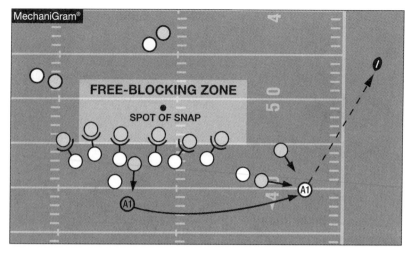

**7-5-2d EXCEPTION 2, TABLE 7-5-2, TABLE 7-5** It is legal for a player to conserve yardage by intentionally throwing an incomplete forward pass if the passer has been beyond the lateral boundary of the free-blocking zone as established at the snap; and the pass reaches the neutral zone, including the extension beyond the sideline. The passer is the only player to possess the ball after the snap ends.

**7-5-7; 7-5-9** Pass interference restrictions apply only beyond the neutral zone and only if the legal forward pass, untouched by the defense in or behind the neutral zone, crosses the neutral zone. The touching by No. 61 makes No. 60 an eligible receiver.

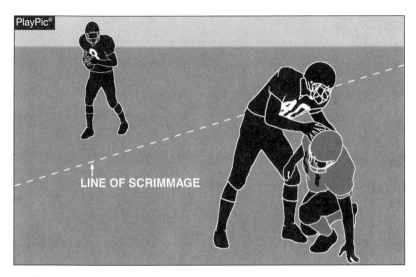

PlayPic®

LINE OF SCRIMMAGE

**7-5-8a; 7-5-10** During a down in which a legal forward pass crossed the neutral zone, a Team A receiver may not contact an opponent with his hands beyond the neutral zone for any purpose until the pass has touched a player. If a forward pass is thrown beyond the neutral zone, the contact results in offensive pass interference. Team A restrictions begin with the snap.

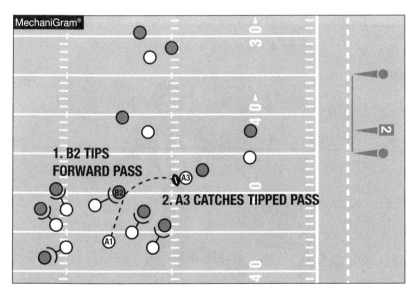

MechaniGram®

**1. B2 TIPS FORWARD PASS**

**2. A3 CATCHES TIPPED PASS**

**7-5-9; 7-5-10** Tipped pass by B2. Lineman A3 is eligible as the pass was tipped by B behind the line of scrimmage Pass restrictions for both A and B ended when B touched the pass.

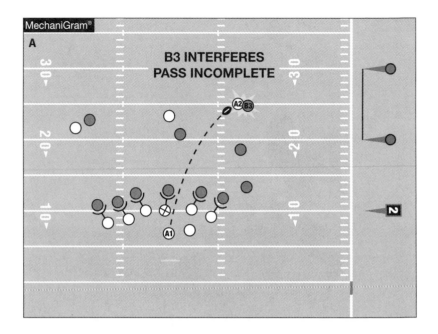

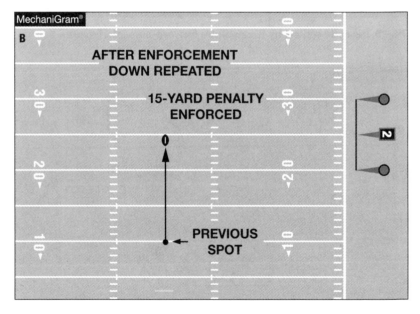

**7-5-10 PENALTY** When B commits pass interference (MechaniGram A), the down is replayed after enforcement of a 15-yard penalty from the previous spot (MechaniGram B).

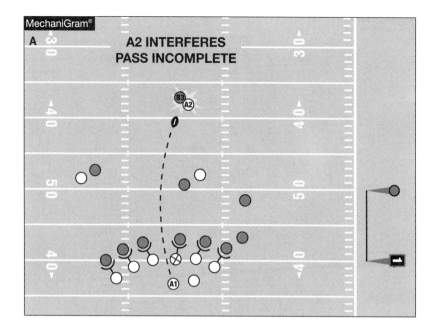

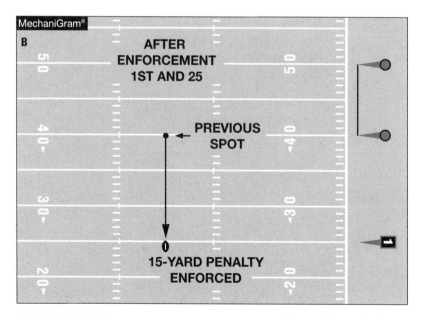

**7-5-10 PENALTY** When A commits pass interference (MechaniGram A), the down is replayed after enforcement of a 15-yard penalty from the previous spot (MechaniGram B).

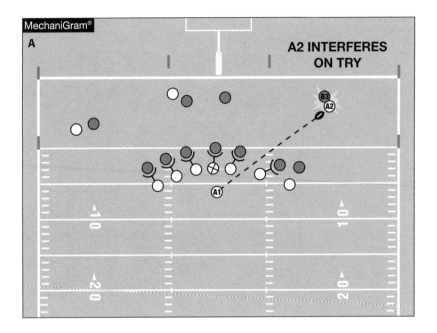

**A**

**A2 INTERFERES ON TRY**

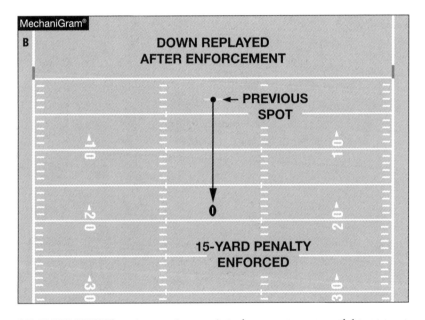

**B**

**DOWN REPLAYED AFTER ENFORCEMENT**

PREVIOUS SPOT

**0**

**15-YARD PENALTY ENFORCED**

**7-5-10 PENALTY** When A commits pass interference on a successful try (MechaniGram A), the down is replayed after enforcement of a 15-yard penalty from the previous spot (MechaniGram B).

**7-5-11a** When two opposing eligible pass receivers are making a simultaneous and bona fide attempt to catch or bat the ball, and there is unavoidable contact, it is not a foul. The defender and receiver both have a right to attempt to gain possession of the pass.

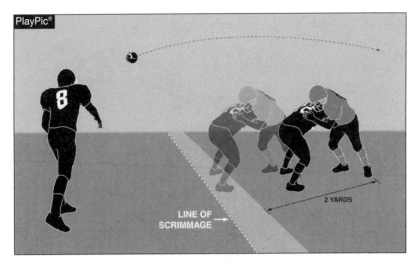

**7-5-12** Ineligible A players may not advance beyond the expanded neutral zone on a legal forward pass play before a legal forward pass that crosses the neutral zone is in flight. The neutral zone expands two yards behind the defensive line of scrimmage following the snap.

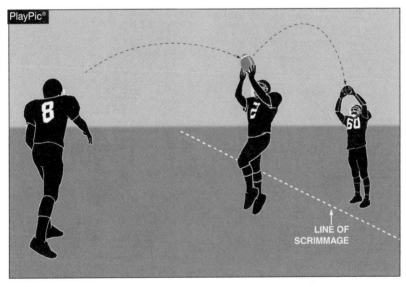

**7-5-12** Ineligible receiver downfield and illegal touching by No. 60 because he was beyond the neutral zone before the legal forward pass which crossed the neutral zone was thrown. On a pass that crosses the neutral zone, touching by A does not make the ineligible receivers eligible.

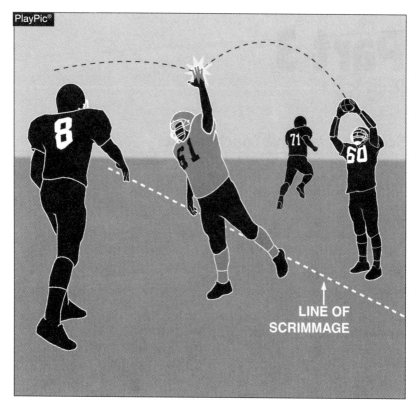

**7-5-12** Ineligible No. 71 is not downfield illegally, due to the fact No. 61 touched the ball prior to the legal forward pass crossing the neutral zone.

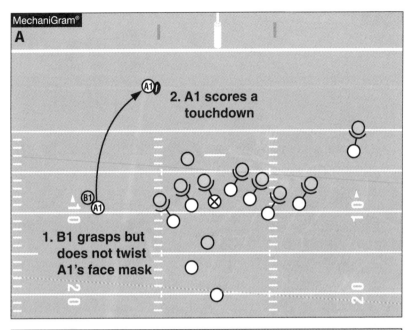

**A**

**2. A1 scores a touchdown**

**1. B1 grasps but does not twist A1's face mask**

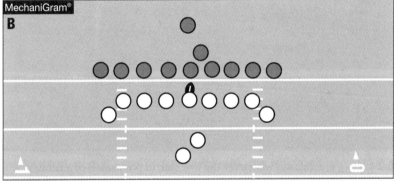

**B**

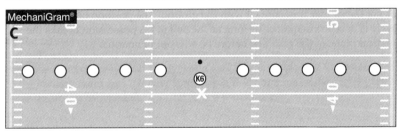

**C**

**8-2-2** A team that is fouled (other than unsportsmanlike conduct or a nonplayer foul) during a play that results in a touchdown (MechaniGram A) may choose to have the penalty for a live-ball foul enforced on the try (MechaniGram B) or the subsequent kickoff (MechaniGram C).

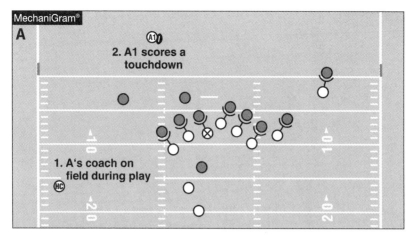

**MechaniGram®**

**A**

(A1) 🏈

**2. A1 scores a touchdown**

**1. A's coach on field during play**

(HC)

**PlayPic®**

**B**

44

52

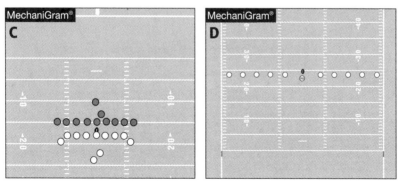

**MechaniGram®**

**C**

**MechaniGram®**

**D**

**8-2-2; 8-2-3; 8-2-4** During a down that results in a touchdown (MechaniGram A), if either team commits an unsportsmanlike (PlayPic B) or nonplayer foul the offended team has the choice of enforcement on the try (MechaniGram C) or the subsequent kickoff (MechaniGram D).

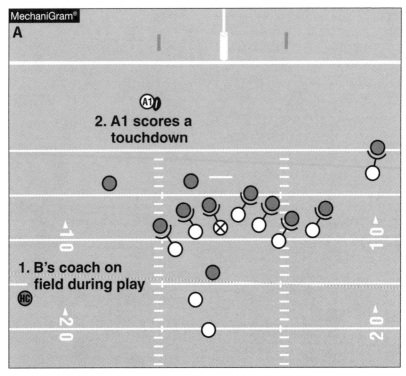

2. A1 scores a
touchdown

1. B's coach on
field during play

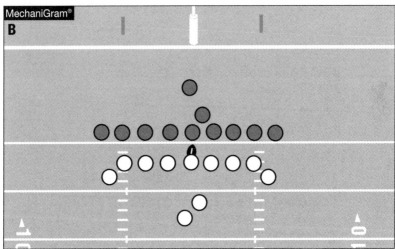

**8-2-2; 8-2-3; 8-2-4; 10-5-1f** If during a touchdown-scoring play on the
last timed down of the fourth period either team commits a foul that has
succeeding-spot enforcement (MechaniGram A), it is not possible to carry over
the penalty to an overtime period. The penalty must be enforced on the try
(Mechanigram B).

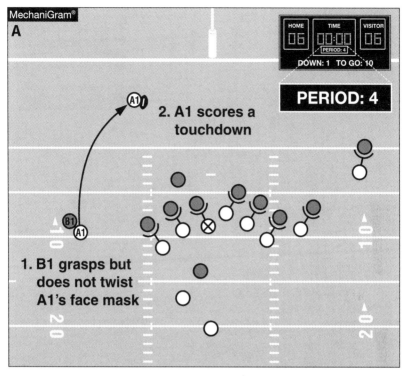

**A**

2. A1 scores a touchdown

HOME
06
TIME
00:00
PERIOD: 4
VISITOR
06
DOWN: 1 TO GO: 10

**PERIOD: 4**

B1

A1

1. B1 grasps but does not twist A1's face mask

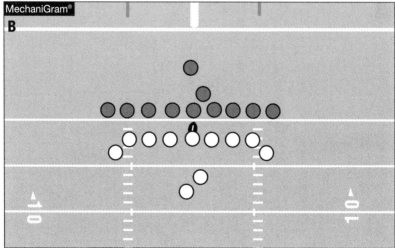

**B**

8-2-2a The opponent of the scoring team commits a live-ball foul (other than unsportsmanlike conduct or a nonplayer foul) during the last timed down of the fourth period and there was no change of possession (MechaniGram A). By rule, the penalty must be enforced on the try (MechaniGram B).

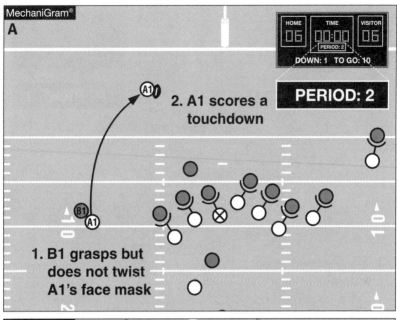

HOME 06 | TIME 00:00 PERIOD: 2 | VISITOR 06

DOWN: 1 TO GO: 10

**2. A1 scores a touchdown**

**PERIOD: 2**

**1. B1 grasps but does not twist A1's face mask**

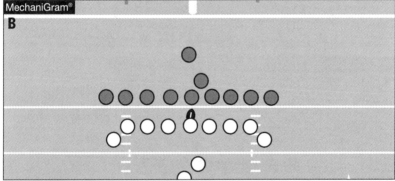

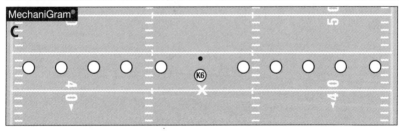

**8-2-2a, b** The opponent of the scoring team commits a live-ball foul (other than unsportsmanlike conduct or a nonplayer foul) during the last timed down of the second period and there was no change of possession (MechaniGram A). The penalty may be enforced on the try (MechaniGram B) or on the subsequent kickoff to start the second half (MechaniGram C).

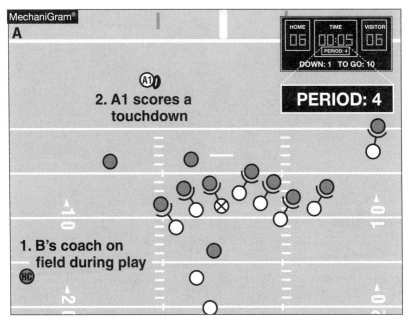

**MechaniGram®**
**A**

2. A1 scores a touchdown

PERIOD: 4

1. B's coach on field during play

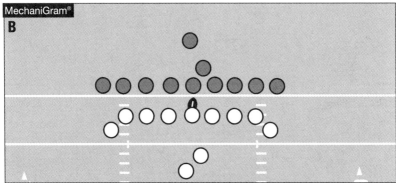

**MechaniGram®**
**B**

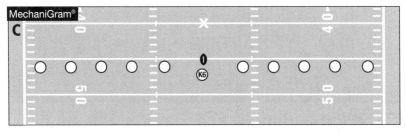

**MechaniGram®**
**C**

**8-2-2a, b; 8-2-3a, b; 8-2-4a, b; 10-5-1f** If during a touchdown-scoring play either team commits a foul that has succeeding-spot enforcement (MechaniGram A), the penalty may be enforced on either the try (MechaniGram B) or on the subsequent kickoff (MechaniGram C).

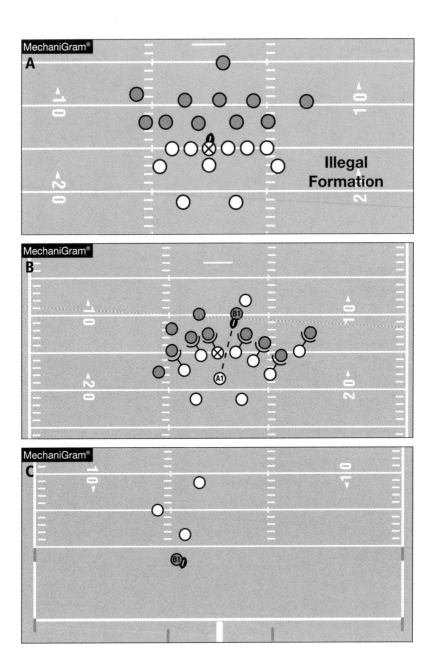

**Illegal Formation**

**8-2-3** If the foul is by A before B gains possession and then scores, B has no penalty options, as it must decline A's foul to keep the score (10-5-3). In MechaniGram A, A is flagged for an illegal formation. A1's pass intercepted (MechaniGram B) and returned for a touchdown (MechaniGram C). If B wants to keep the score, it must decline the penalty. There is no option for enforcement on the subsequent kickoff.

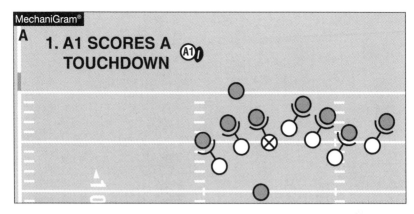

**A**

### 1. A1 SCORES A TOUCHDOWN

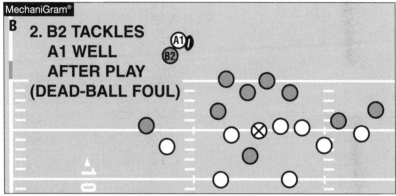

**B**

### 2. B2 TACKLES A1 WELL AFTER PLAY (DEAD-BALL FOUL)

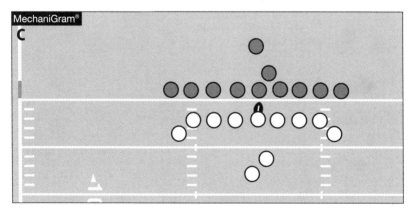

**C**

**8-2-5** The optional penalty enforcement applies on dead-ball fouls that occur prior to the initial ready-for-play on the try. In MechaniGram A, A1 scores a touchdown. Several seconds after the play is over, B2 contacts A1 (MechaniGram B). A has the option to have the penalty enforced from the succeeding spot or on the the subsequent kickoff. Enforcement on the try would result in half-the-distance enforcement (MechaniGram C).

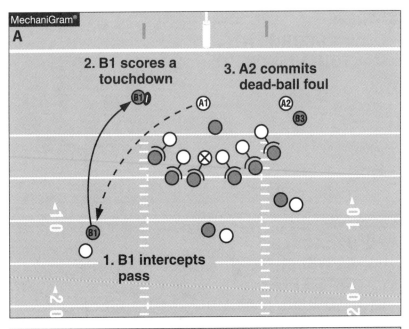

**A**

2. B1 scores a touchdown

3. A2 commits dead-ball foul

1. B1 intercepts pass

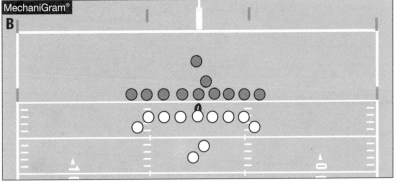

**B**

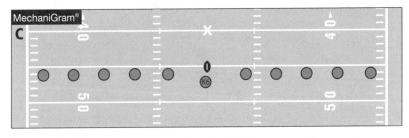

**C**

**8-2-5; 10-5-1f** If either team commits a foul that has succeeding-spot enforcement before the initial ready-for-play signal on the ensuing try following a touchdown-scoring play (MechaniGram A), the penalty may be enforced on either the try (MechaniGram B) or on the subsequent kickoff (MechaniGram C).

**8-3-2b** When it is apparent a kick will not score during a try, the ball becomes dead immediately. The kick cannot score after the kicked ball touches the ground. There's no way A or B can score any points once the kick fails. Game officials must be aware that after a blocked field-goal attempt, which is not a try, the ball remains live.

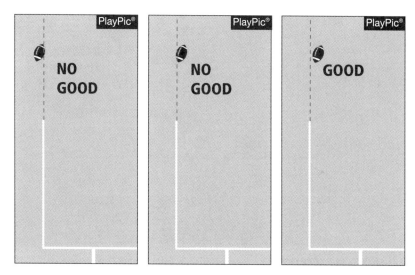

**8-4-1** During a field-goal attempt, the kick must pass above the crossbar and between the vertical uprights or the inside edges of the uprights extended in order to be successful. If any part of the ball penetrates the plane of the inside edges of the vertical-uprights extended, it is unsuccessful.

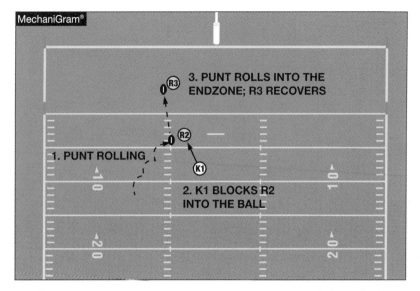

1. PUNT ROLLING

3. PUNT ROLLS INTO THE ENDZONE; R3 RECOVERS

2. K1 BLOCKS R2 INTO THE BALL

**8-5-1b** K1 blocks R2 into the ball. The accidental touching of a loose ball by a player who was blocked into the ball by an opponent is ignored and does not constitute a new force. The result of this play is a touchback.

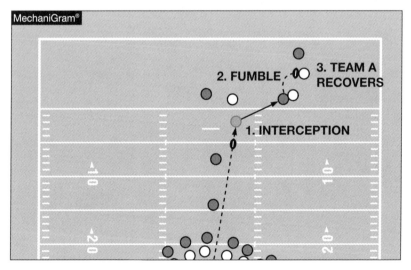

2. FUMBLE

3. TEAM A RECOVERS

1. INTERCEPTION

**8-2-1b, 8-5-2a EXCEPTION** The Team B player intercepts (1). His original momentum carries him into his own end zone after a catch inside his 5-yard line. If the fumble is recovered by Team A in Team B's end zone (3), it is a touchdown for Team A.

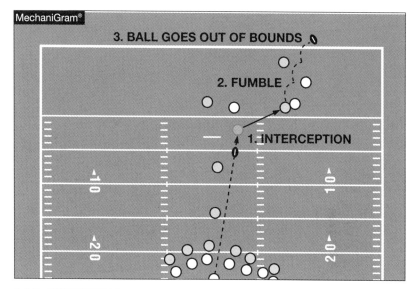

**MechaniGram®**

**3. BALL GOES OUT OF BOUNDS**

**2. FUMBLE**

**1. INTERCEPTION**

**8-5-2a EXCEPTION** The Team B player intercepts (1). His original momentum carries him into his own end zone after a catch inside his 5-yard line. If the fumble goes out of bounds behind the goal line (3), it belongs to Team B on the yard line on which it was intercepted.

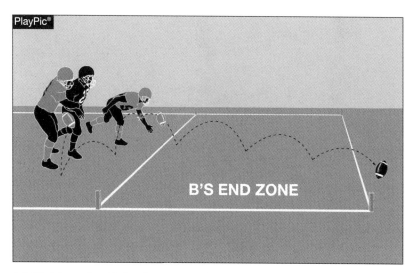

**PlayPic®**

**B'S END ZONE**

**8-5-2b** After a fumble has been grounded, a new force may result from a muff or bat. If the covering official rules B's attempted recovery provided a new force causing the ball to go into and through his own end zone, the result is a safety. If B had not added a new force, A's fumble through B's end zone would have been a touchback.

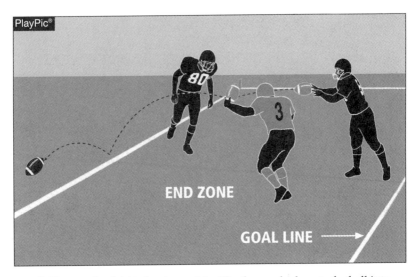

**8-5-2b** The result of this play is a safety. The force which puts the ball into the end zone is the backward pass No. 3 did not supply a new force as the backward pass had not been grounded when he contacted it.

**8-5-2b** One receiver blocks the punt and the ball is rolling near the goal line when a teammate touches the ball in an attempt to recover. The covering official must judge whether the ball could have gone into the end zone without the touch. Since no new force was given, the original force was supplied by the kick and it is a safety if the ball goes out of bounds from the end zone.

**8-5-2c** After muffing the snap, No. 11 holds No. 58 to prevent him from recovering the ball. This is a foul by No. 11, for which the penalty is administered toward the end line from the basic spot as defined in Rule 10-4. The result is a safety. If No. 58 had recovered in the end zone, A's foul could have been declined resulting in a touchdown.

**8-5-3c** It is a touchback when a fumble is the force which sends the ball from the field of play across the opponent's goal line and the opponent is in possession in the end zone when the ball becomes dead. If the ball is fumbled through the end zone and out of bounds, it also results in a touchback. If A had recovered in the end zone, it would have been a touchback.

PlayPic®

END ZONE

**8-5-3d** A forward pass is the force which causes the ball to cross the opponent's goal line. Following the interception by B, if the ball becomes dead in Team B's possession in the end zone, the result is a touchback B may run the ball out of the end zone or may down it in the end zone. If B fumbles and A recovers in the end zone, it is a touchdown for A.

# Part 3
Rule 9

## Conduct of Players and Others

It must be recognized that participation in sports requires an acceptance of risk of injury. Football is a vigorous, physical contact game and, for this reason, much attention is given to minimizing the risk of injury to the players. In addition to requiring player equipment which offers protection, those responsible for administering the program must be certain coaches teach techniques which are within the rules. Game officials must accept the responsibility for properly administering the rules as written.

In a game in which forceful, physical contact is not only permitted but encouraged, there will invariably be some injury. However, when injury results from techniques taught for the purpose of physically abusing opponents, such techniques must be eliminated.

Blocking by a player either on offense or defense is legal provided it is not: kick-catching interference; forward-pass interference; a personal foul or prohibited contact such as a chop block, etc. Except to bring down the runner, blocking below the waist is legal only if the player(s) is/are on the line of scrimmage and in the zone at the snap, the block is in the free-blocking zone and the block is an immediate, initial action following the snap. A receiver who gives a valid or invalid signal for a fair catch may not block until the kick has ended.

In order to ensure balance between the offense and defense, definite restrictions are placed upon each. An offensive player is restricted in the use of his hands and arms other than in a legal block. A defensive player may use his hands to push or pull an opponent in order to get at a runner or to ward off a blocker or to reach a loose ball which he may retain following possession. It is always a foul for a player on either team to lock his hands while contacting an opponent with his hands or to strike an opponent with the hand, forearm or elbow.

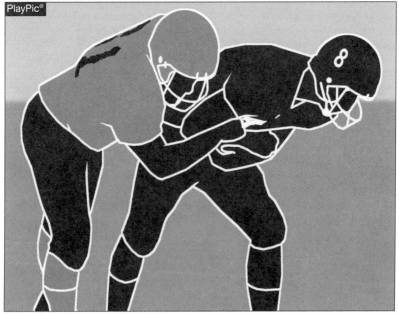

**9-2-3c** This contact by No. 61 is not a foul since No. 8 is pretending to be a runner. However, the defensive player must exercise reasonable caution in avoiding any unnecessary tackle. A runner or player pretending to be a runner may be contacted from the front or back.

**9-2-3d** When No. 80 is no longer a potential blocker, contacting the receiver is illegal use of the hands by the defense. Once No. 80 is on the same yard line as the defender, or after he has made his cut away from the defender, he is no longer a potential blocker. If this contact occurs after a forward pass which crosses the neutral zone is in flight, it is defensive pass interference, unless the pass is not in the vicinity of the contact.

**9-3-2** The block is legal, even though contact is below the waist. The restriction on blocking below the waist does not apply unless the opponent had one or both feet on the ground. No. 75 has caused the contact to be below the waist when he jumped in an attempt to block the kick.

**9-3-5b** The offensive blocker is between the runner and the potential tackler. The defender pushes the blocker from behind above the waist, then continues to pursue and make the tackle. The contact by the defender on the blocker is legal. It is also legal to use hands on the back of an opponent when the ball is loose and the player may legally recover it.

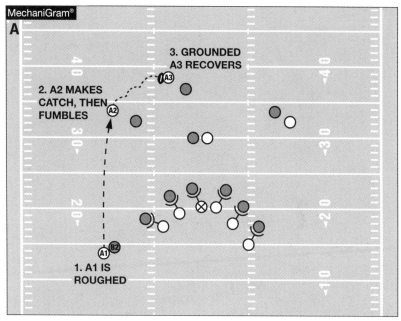

**A**

3. GROUNDED
A3 RECOVERS

2. A2 MAKES
CATCH, THEN
FUMBLES

1. A1 IS
ROUGHED

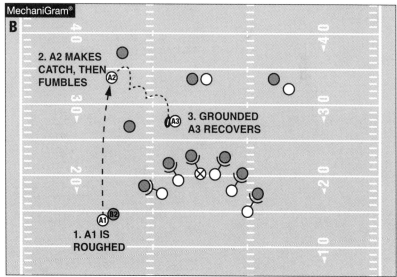

**B**

2. A2 MAKES
CATCH, THEN
FUMBLES

3. GROUNDED
A3 RECOVERS

1. A1 IS
ROUGHED

**9-4 PENALTY** For the purpose of roughing the passer, the last spot where A possesses the ball (by run or recovery) is the spot from which to enforce the roughing. In MechaniGram A, A1 is roughed as A2 catches a pass at A's 35-yard line, where he fumbles. Grounded A3 recovers at A's 39-yard line. Enforcement is from A's 39-yard line, which is where the ball was recovered by A. In MechaniGram B, A2's fumble is recovered by grounded A3 at A's 28-yard line. The penalty enforced from the spot of recovery.

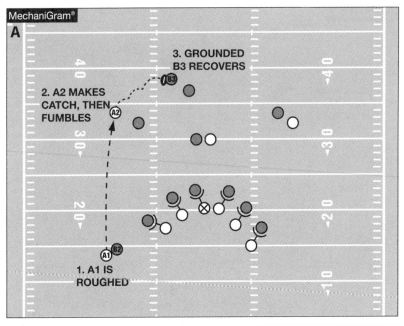

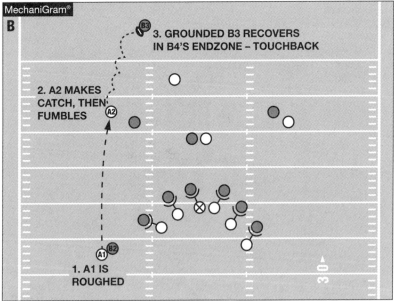

**9-4 PENALTY** When the passer is roughed and there is a change of team possession or the run ends behind the previous spot, the penalty is enforced from the previous spot. In MechaniGram A, because B recovers the fumble, enforcement is from the previous spot. In MechaniGram B, when the result of the play is a touchback, enforcement is from the previous spot.

**9-4-3b** The rules provide that it is illegal to contact a player who is clearly out of the play or to make any other contact which is deemed unnecessary and which incites roughness. Also, unwarranted and unnecessary "punishing" of a ball carrier must be eliminated.

**9-4-3g** No player or nonplayer shall make any other contact with an opponent, including a defenseless player, which is deemed unnecessary or excessive and which incites roughness.

**9-4-3h PENALTY** Grasping the face mask, helmet opening, chin strap or tooth and mouth protector attached to the face mask is a foul. If there is twisting, turning or pulling of the face mask (PlayPic A), helmet opening, chin strap or tooth and mouth protector attached to a face mask, it is a 15-yard penalty; otherwise it is a 5-yard penalty for incidental grasping of the face mask (PlayPic B). When in doubt, it is a 15-yard penalty.

**9-4-3h** Grasping an opponent's tooth and mouth protector attached to the face mask is a foul.

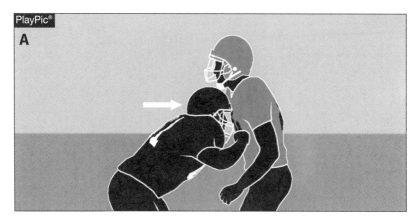

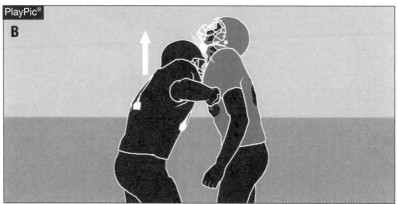

**9-4-3i** Butt blocking (PlayPics A and B) and face tackling (PlayPic C) are both tactics which involve initiating contact with the helmet directly into an opponent in blocking or tackling respectively. Both result in a foul for illegal helmet contact.

**9-4-3j** Striking blows are always illegal. This example of a "clotheslining" tactic by a defensive back must be penalized. The penalty of 15 yards will be measured from the end of the run and the offender shall be disqualified. Tactics such as this have no place in the game.

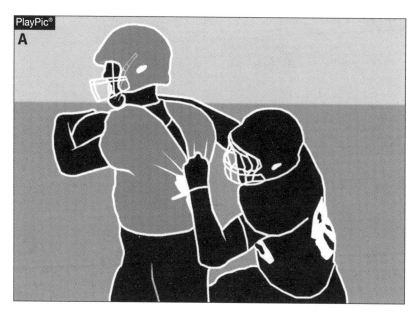

**9-4-3k** No player or nonplayer shall grab the inside back or side collar or the name plate area (directly below the back collar), of either the shoulder pads or the jersey of the runner and subsequently pull (backward or sideward) that opponent to the ground (horse-collar), even if possession is lost. The horse-collar foul is enforced as a live-ball foul.

**9-4-3k** If one would-be tackler has grabbed the shoulder pads or collar of the runner, but that opponent is brought down as the result of a more conventional tackle by another player, there is no foul.

**9-4-3k** If the horse-collar tackle (PlayPic A) is not completed until after the runner crosses B's goal line or a sideline (PlayPic B), it is enforced as a live-ball foul. Team A may choose enforcement of the 15-yard penalty on the try or on the subsequent kickoff.

**PlayPic®**

**A**

**FOURTH DOWN**

**PlayPic®**

**B**

**FOURTH DOWN**

**9-4-3k** The horse-collar is to be enforced as a live-ball foul. In PlayPic A, the horse-collar was initiated inbounds but ends out of bounds short of the line-to-gain PlayPic B. That is a live-ball foul carrying a 15-yard penalty. Enforcement on the play illustrated will result in a first down for A.

**9-4-3k** The name plate area (directly below the back collar) has been added to the criteria for an illegal horse-collar tackle. It is a foul to grab the inside back, name plate area or side collar of either the shoulder pads or the jersey of the runner and subsequently pull (backwards or sideward) that opponent to the ground, even if possession is lost. The horse-collar is enforced as a live-ball foul.

**9-4-3l** It is a personal foul if a player or nonplayer initiates contact with an opposing player whose helmet has come completely off.

**9-4-4** Defensive players must make a definite effort to avoid charging into a passer, who has thrown the ball from in or behind the neutral zone, after it is clear the ball has been thrown. No defensive player shall commit any illegal personal contact foul listed in 9-4-3 against the passer. Grasping and twisting of the face mask as seen in the PlayPic is considered roughing the passer.

**9-4 PENALTY** Number 54 grasps but does not twist, pull or turn the passer's face mask. The foul is for an incidental face mask, and is not roughing the passer. The penalty is five yards administered from the basic spot as defined in Rule 10-4, and no automatic first down.

**9-4-5** In PlayPic A, the R player makes only slight contact with the kicker, which only causes the kicker to spin around (PlayPic B). The covering official could judge no foul on this play.

**9-4-5** In PlayPic A, the R player makes contact with the kicker, which causes the kicker to be displaced (PlayPic B). This is intended to illustrate running into the kicker.

**9-4-5** In PlayPic A, the R player contacts the kicker's plant leg, making the kicker extremely vulnerable. The contact knocks the kicker to the ground (PlayPic B). This is an example of roughing the kicker.

PlayPic®
A

PlayPic®
B

PlayPic®
C

PlayPic®
D

**9-4-5** In PlayPic A, the kicker takes the snap. Another K player blocks an onrushing R player (PlayPic B). The block causes the R player to contact the kicker (PlayPic C), knocking him to the ground (PlayPic D). Because K's block caused R's contact on the kicker, there is no foul.

**BAD SNAP**

**9-4-5** A 15-yard penalty is applicable when there is illegal contact on the kicker/holder. The penalty also carries an automatic first down. A bad snap does not automatically eliminate the kicker's protection from roughing.

**9-4-7** No defensive player may use the hand(s) to slap a blocker's head (PlayPic A). In (PlayPic B), if the slap is to the head while the ball is in the air to pass, it would be defensive pass interference.

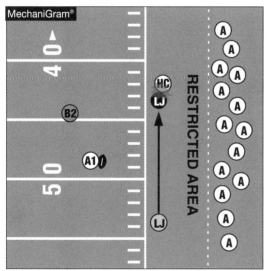

**9-4-8 PENALTY** If a game official and a nonplayer unintentionally collide in the restricted area while the ball is live, the offended team is penalized 15 yards for illegal personal contact. A second offense would result in ejection of the head coach and a 15-yard penalty from the succeeding spot.

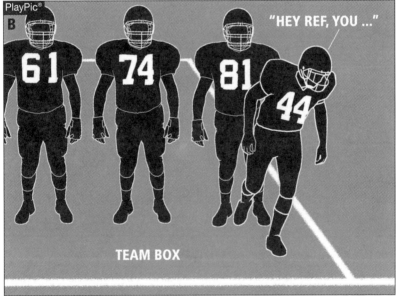

"HEY REF, YOU ..."

TEAM BOX

**9-5; 9-8 PENALTY** No. 44 receives one unsportsmanlike foul for spiking the ball as a player in PlayPic A and a second for foul language as a nonplayer in PlayPic B No. 44 is disqualified upon receiving the second unsportsmanlike foul which carries a 15-yard penalty. Game officials must keep accurate records of unsportsmanlike fouls.

**9-5-1c** Players must be penalized for prolonged or excessive acts designed to focus attention on themselves. Such displays must be penalized without hesitation. The unsportsmanlike act is penalized from the succeeding spot.

**9-6-1** Team A receiver No. 80 steps on the sideline and then returns inbounds and catches a forward pass. No. 80 has committed an illegal-participation foul. The spot of the foul is the spot where he returned inbounds. No foul if he does not return inbounds. Similar restrictions apply to Team K players.

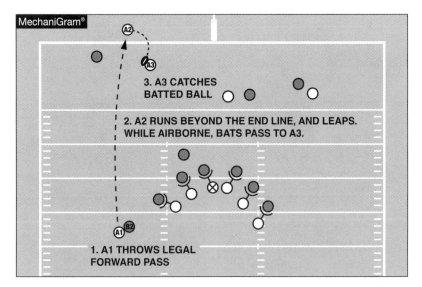

3. A3 CATCHES BATTED BALL

2. A2 RUNS BEYOND THE END LINE, AND LEAPS. WHILE AIRBORNE, BATS PASS TO A3.

1. A1 THROWS LEGAL FORWARD PASS

**9-6-2** It is illegal participation if a player intentionally goes out of bounds during the down and returns to the field, intentionally touches the ball, influences the play, or otherwise participates. The penalty is 15 yards from the previous spot.

**9-6-4g** If a player whose helmet comes completely off during a down continues to participate beyond the immediate action in which the player is engaged, it is a foul for illegal participation.

**9-7-2 EXCEPTION** K may bat a scrimmage kick which is beyond the neutral zone toward his own goal line. This is legal action. If the bat occurred beyond the plane of the goal line, the ball was already dead, causing it to be a touchback. K may also bat a scrimmage kick in flight beyond the neutral zone toward his own goal line if no R player is in position to catch the ball.

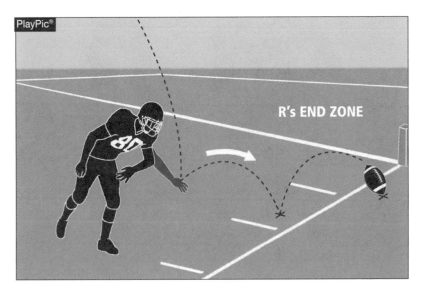

**9-7-2 EXCEPTION** When the ball is beyond the neutral zone and no Team R player is in position to catch the ball, Team K players may only bat the kick backward (toward their own goal line). Batting the ball forward is a foul.

**9-8-1** A second unsportsmanlike foul with a 15-yard penalty by the same member of the coaching staff will cause the coach to be disqualified and removed from the stadium area. He may not communicate with coaches or players from the area or from the press box, he may not be in the team locker room during the halftime intermission and must adhere to state association rules upon disqualification.

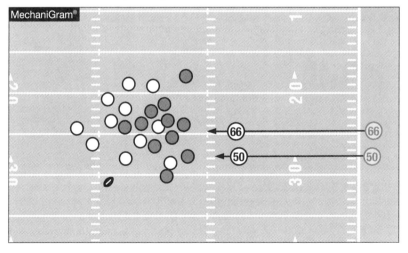

**9-8-1l** While a fight is taking place on the field, two substitutes of Team A leave their team box and then enter the field. The two substitutes are each charged with an unsportsmanlike conduct foul and are also disqualified. Two 15-yard penalties will be assessed. Substitutes shall not leave the team box during a fight. In addition, the players who are fighting shall be penalized and disqualified.

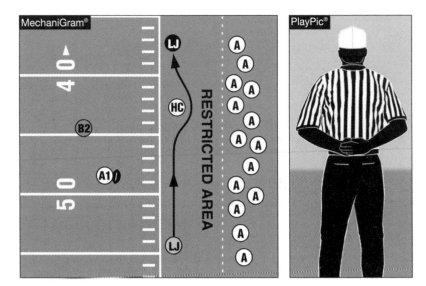

**9-8-3** If a player, coach or nonplayer is in the restricted zone while the ball is live but does not contact a game official, a warning is issued for the first offense. The second instance results in a five-yard penalty and each subsequent offense results in a 15-yard unsportsmanlike conduct penalty.

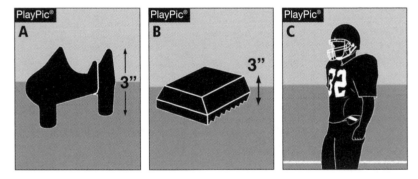

**9-9-3; 9-9-4; 9-9 PENALTY** Use of kicking tees that elevate the lowest point of the ball more than two inches (PlayPics A and B) results in a 15-yard penalty from the basic spot as defined in Rule 10-4. Hiding the ball under a jersey (PlayPic C) is also an unfair act. The penalty is 15 yards from the basic spot as defined in Rule 10-4.

# Part 3
## Rule 10

## Enforcement of Penalties

In the NFHS football rules, the penalty-enforcement philosophy is based upon the principle that a team is entitled to the advantage of distance gained without the assistance of a foul. If a foul occurs during a down, the basic spot is determined by the type of play and applicable rule. There are two types of plays:

1. A loose-ball play is action during:
    a. free kick or scrimmage kick.
    b. a legal forward pass.
    c. a backward pass (including the snap), illegal kick or a fumble made by A from in or behind the neutral zone prior to a change of team possession.
    d. A loose-ball play also includes the run (or runs) which precedes such legal or illegal kick, legal forward pass, backward pass or fumble.

2. A running play is any action not included in item 1.

If a foul occurs during a loose-ball play, the basic spot is the previous spot with the exception of post-scrimmage kick fouls. For a running play, the basic spot is defined in Rule 10-4.

While it is possible to have several running plays during a down, with each one having its own basic spot — where the related run ended — there can be only one loose-ball play, during a down.

If a live-ball foul is followed by a dead-ball foul, the penalty for the live-ball foul will be administered from the basic spot as defined in Rule 10-4. The dead-ball foul penalty will then be measured from the succeeding spot. The penalty for any nonplayer or unsportsmanlike foul is administered from the succeeding spot. When there is a double foul during the down, the penalties offset and, in effect, there is no acceptance or declination of them.

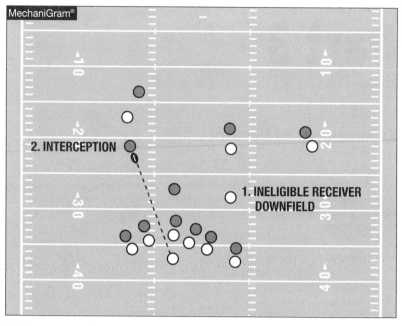

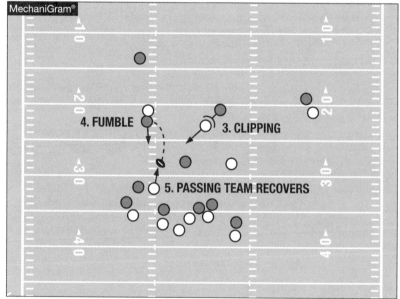

**10-2-1b** This is a double foul. The team gaining final possession had fouled prior to gaining final possession. The penalties cancel and the down will be replayed from the previous spot. When a double foul occurs, the captains are not consulted since the penalties offset automatically even in those cases where the penalty distances are not the same.

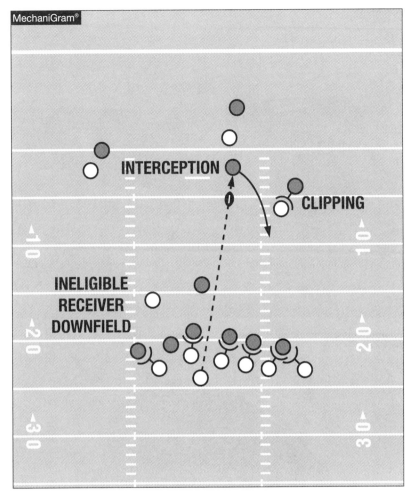

**10-2-2** Live-ball fouls by opponents do not always combine to make a double foul. When there is a change of team possession and the team gaining final possession has not fouled prior to gaining possession and declines the penalty for its opponent's foul, that team may retain possession. If B declines the foul for A's ineligible receiver downfield, B will put the ball in play first and 10 following the administration of the penalty for clipping.

**10-2-5** In PlayPic A, the A player false starts. In PlayPic B, the B player commits a dead-ball personal foul. Both fouls occur before the next live ball. The penalties do not cancel and are enforced in the order of occurrence.

**10-2-5** In PlayPic A, a B player commits a dead-ball personal foul. In PlayPic B, A's coach is flagged for unsportsmanlike conduct. All fouls occur before the completion of any enforcement. The fouls offset and it will be third down.

**10-2-5** In PlayPic A, the B player hits the runner out-of-bounds, a dead-ball foul. In PlayPic B, two A players commit unsportsmanlike fouls. All fouls occur before the completion of any enforcement. One A foul and the B foul offset. The penalty for the remaining A foul is enforced.

**INTENTIONALLY GROUNDING BALL**

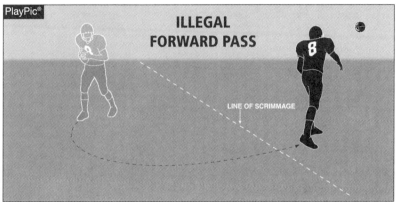

**ILLEGAL FORWARD PASS**

LINE OF SCRIMMAGE

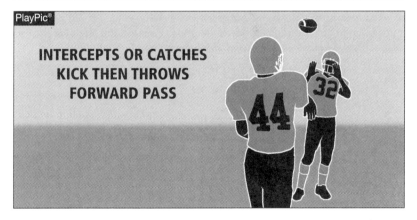

**INTERCEPTS OR CATCHES KICK THEN THROWS FORWARD PASS**

**10-4-4** Since all illegal forward passes are running plays, the penalty, if accepted in any of these plays, will be enforced the basic spot as defined in Rule 10-4. The down will count unless the forward pass was thrown after a change of possession during the down. Following a change of possession, a loss-of-down penalty has no significance.

**FIELD GOAL IS GOOD**

**10-5** If Team K takes the field goal, the penalty for roughing will be enforced from the succeeding spot. Team K may instead accept the penalty resulting in an automatic first down, plus the distance penalty, which could put them in position to go for a touchdown. If the foul is flagrant, the offender is disqualified whether or not the penalty is accepted.

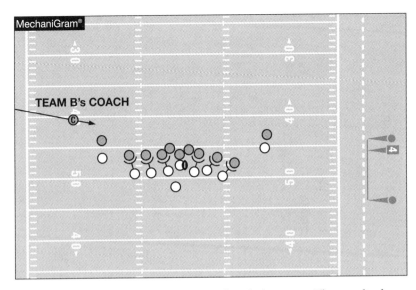

**10-5** Team A is short of a first down on a fourth-down run. The penalty for the dead-ball unsportsmanlike foul on the Team B coach is administered before the line to gain is established for Team B. It will be first and 10 for B from its own 33-yard line.

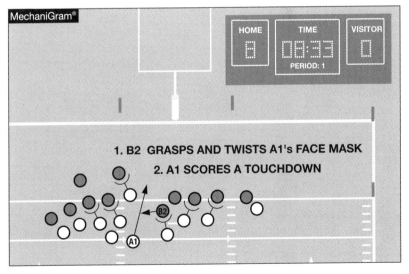

| HOME | TIME | VISITOR |
|:---:|:---:|:---:|
| 8 | 08:33 | 0 |
| | PERIOD: 1 | |

1. B2 GRASPS AND TWISTS A1's FACE MASK

2. A1 SCORES A TOUCHDOWN

**10-5-1f; 8-2-2** If a live-ball defensive foul occurs during a touchdown-scoring play when there is no change of possession, the scoring team may accept the results of the play and have the penalty enforced from the succeeding spot or on the subsequent kickoff.

| 1 Ball ready for play *Untimed down | 2 Start clock | 3 Time-out Discretionary or injury time-out (followed by tapping hands on chest) |
| --- | --- | --- |
| 4 TV/radio time-out | 5 Touchdown, Field goal, Point(s) after touchdown | 6 Safety | 7 Dead ball foul, Touchback (move side to side) |
| 8 First down | 9 Loss of down | 10 Incomplete forward pass Penalty declined No play, no score Toss option deferred | 11 Legal touching of forward pass or scrimmage kick | 12 Inadvertent whistle |
| 13 Disregard flag | 14 End of period | 15 Sideline warning | 16 First touching Illegal touching | 17 Reset play clock to 25 seconds (Use both hands to have play clock reset to 40 seconds) |
| 18 Encroachment | 19 False start Illegal formation Free kick infraction | 20 Illegal shift (2 hands) Illegal motion (1 hand) | 21 Delay of game | 22 Substitution infraction |

PlayPic® PlayPics courtesy of REFEREE (www.referee.com)

# NFHS OFFICIAL FOOTBALL SIGNALS

| | | | | |
|---|---|---|---|---|
| **23** Disconcerting act | **24** Illegal helmet contact Targeting | **25** Illegal horse-collar tackle | **26** Illegal blindside block | **27** Unsportsmanlike conduct Noncontact foul |
| **28** Illegal participation | **29** Sideline interference (Face press box) | **30** Running into or Roughing kicker or holder | **31** Illegal batting/kicking (Followed by pointing toward toe for kicking) | **32** Invalid fair catch Illegal fair catch signal |
| **33** Forward pass interference Kick catching interference | **34** Roughing passer | **35** Illegal pass/forward handing (Face press box) | **36** Intentional grounding | **37** Ineligible downfield on pass |
| **38** Personal foul | **39** Clipping | **40** Blocking below waist | **41** Chop block | **42** Holding/ obstruction Illegal use of hands/arms |
| **43** Illegal block | **44** Helping runner Interlocked blocking | **45** Grasping face mask or helmet opening | **46** Tripping | **47** Disqualification |

PlayPic® PlayPics courtesy of **REFEREE** (www.referee.com)

*2023 Football Rules Simplified & Illustrated* **267**

| Double stakes | 11 players | Snapper protection | Unbalanced line |
|---|---|---|---|
| Indicates that more than ten yards to go before first down, to prevent accidental stopping of clock. | Fist extended straight out with elbow not bent and the thumb up in fist, indication of 11 players in game when counting complete. | Indicates to each other (R and U) that this play requires protection for snapper in accordance with rules. | Hand on cheek, indicating unbalanced line to trigger all to look for ineligibles and umpire to check numbering. Also used for indicating two or more players or no players outside the tackle on the line of scrimmage. |

**Start clock on snap**

Arms crossed at wrists in front of waist. Last play was out of bounds (start clock on snap).

**Backward pass**

Given by R unless immediately thrown after snap in which case wing has crew option to signal. NO signal if forward. Also, same signal by wing officials to indicate player nearest wing official is off the line of scrimmage.

**Play ends inbounds**

Start clock on ready.

**Five second count**

Visible count by R (Four-Game Officials Crew) and BJ (Five-Game Officials Crew) of the last five seconds when on-field play clocks are not utilized.

**PlayPic®** PlayPics courtesy of **REFEREE** (www.referee.com)

# 2023 NFHS FOOTBALL RULES PENALTY SUMMARY

**LOSS OF 5 YARDS**                                                     **SIGNAL**

Delay of game. . . . . . . . . . . . . . . . . . . . . . . . . . . . . . . . . . . . . . . . . . . . 7-21

Illegal substitution. . . . . . . . . . . . . . . . . . . . . . . . . . . . . . . . . . . . . . . . . . 22

Free-kick infraction . . . . . . . . . . . . . . . . . . . . . . . . . . . . . . . . . . . . . . . 7-19

Encroachment. . . . . . . . . . . . . . . . . . . . . . . . . . . . . . . . . . . . . . . . . . . . 7-18

Free kick out of bounds . . . . . . . . . . . . . . . . . . . . . . . . . . . . . . . . . . . . . 19

Invalid or illegal fair-catch signal. . . . . . . . . . . . . . . . . . . . . . . . . . . . . . 32

Snap infraction . . . . . . . . . . . . . . . . . . . . . . . . . . . . . . . . . . . . . . . . . . . 7-19

False start. . . . . . . . . . . . . . . . . . . . . . . . . . . . . . . . . . . . . . . . . . . . . . . . 7-19

Disconcerting act . . . . . . . . . . . . . . . . . . . . . . . . . . . . . . . . . . . . . . . . . . 7-23

Illegal formation. . . . . . . . . . . . . . . . . . . . . . . . . . . . . . . . . . . . . . . . . . . . 19

Less than five players on A's line or numbering violation. . . . . . . . . . . . . . . . 19

Illegal shift or illegal motion . . . . . . . . . . . . . . . . . . . . . . . . . . . . . . . . . . . 20

Planned loose-ball infraction . . . . . . . . . . . . . . . . . . . . . . . . . . . . . . . . . . . 19

Illegally handing ball forward (also loss of down) . . . . . . . . . . . . . . . . . . . 35-9

Illegal forward pass (by A) (also loss of down) . . . . . . . . . . . . . . . . . . . . . 35-9

Illegal forward pass (by B). . . . . . . . . . . . . . . . . . . . . . . . . . . . . . . . . . . . . 35

Intentional grounding (also loss of down). . . . . . . . . . . . . . . . . . . . . . . . . . 36-9

Ineligible receiver illegally downfield . . . . . . . . . . . . . . . . . . . . . . . . . . . . . 37

Illegal touching (also loss of down). . . . . . . . . . . . . . . . . . . . . . . . . . . . . . 16-9

Helping runner . . . . . . . . . . . . . . . . . . . . . . . . . . . . . . . . . . . . . . . . . . . . 44

Incidental grasping of opponent's face mask (or any helmet opening, chin strap
or attached tooth and mouth protector). . . . . . . . . . . . . . . . . . . . . . . . . . . . 45

Running into kicker/holder . . . . . . . . . . . . . . . . . . . . . . . . . . . . . . . . . . . . 30

Sideline interference . . . . . . . . . . . . . . . . . . . . . . . . . . . . . . . . . . . . . . . . 7-29

Attendant illegally on field . . . . . . . . . . . . . . . . . . . . . . . . . . . . . . . . . . . . 19

Nonplayer outside of the team box, but not on field . . . . . . . . . . . . . . . . . . . 7-29

**LOSS OF 10 YARDS**

Illegally kicking or batting ball. . . . . . . . . . . . . . . . . . . . . . . . . . . . . . . . . . 31

Illegal blocking technique . . . . . . . . . . . . . . . . . . . . . . . . . . . . . . . . . . . . . 42

Interlocked blocking. . . . . . . . . . . . . . . . . . . . . . . . . . . . . . . . . . . . . . . . . 44

Holding . . . . . . . . . . . . . . . . . . . . . . . . . . . . . . . . . . . . . . . . . . . . . . . . . 42

Runner grasping a teammate . . . . . . . . . . . . . . . . . . . . . . . . . . . . . . . . . . 42

Illegal use of hands or arms . . . . . . . . . . . . . . . . . . . . . . . . . . . . . . . . . . . 42

Illegal block in the back . . . . . . . . . . . . . . . . . . . . . . . . . . . . . . . . . . . . . . 43

Illegal block on free kick. . . . . . . . . . . . . . . . . . . . . . . . . . . . . . . . . . . . . . 43

## LOSS OF 15 YARDS

## DISQUALIFICATION ASSOCIATED WITH CERTAIN 15-YARD PENALTIES

# NFHS PUBLICATIONS

### Prices effective April 1, 2023 — March 31, 2024

## RULES PUBLICATIONS

| | |
|---|---|
| Baseball Rules Book......................................$12.00 | Boys Lacrosse Rules Book..........................$12.00 |
| Baseball Case Book......................................$12.00 | Girls Lacrosse Rules Book...........................$12.00 |
| Baseball Umpires Manual (2023 & 2024).....$12.00 | Soccer Rules Book.......................................$12.00 |
| Baseball Simplified & Illustrated Rules ........$15.95 | Softball Rules Book......................................$12.00 |
| Basketball Rules Book..................................$12.00 | Softball Case Book......................................$12.00 |
| Basketball Case Book...................................$12.00 | Softball Umpires Manual (2024 & 2025)......$12.00 |
| Basketball Simplified & Illustrated Rules ......$15.95 | Softball Simplified & Illustrated Rules .........$15.95 |
| Basketball Officials Manual (2023-25) ..........$12.00 | Spirit Rules Book.........................................$12.00 |
| Basketball Handbook (2022-24)....................$12.00 | Swimming & Diving Rules Book ...................$12.00 |
| Field Hockey Rules Book...............................$12.00 | Track & Field Rules Book.............................$12.00 |
| Football Rules Book .....................................$12.00 | Track & Field Case Book .............................$12.00 |
| Football Case Book......................................$12.00 | Track & Field Manual (2023 & 2024)............$12.00 |
| Football Simplified & Illustrated Rules ..........$15.95 | Volleyball Rules Book...................................$12.00 |
| Football Handbook (2023 & 2024)................$12.00 | Volleyball Case Book & Manual....................$12.00 |
| Football Game Officials Manual (2022 & 2023).$12.00 | Volleyball Simplified & Illustrated Rules .......$15.95 |
| Girls Gymnastics Rules Book & Manual | Water Polo Rules Book (2022-24) ................$12.00 |
| (2022-24)...............................................$12.00 | Wrestling Rules Book...................................$12.00 |
| Ice Hockey Rules Book ................................$12.00 | Wrestling Case Book & Manual....................$12.00 |

## MISCELLANEOUS ITEMS

| | |
|---|---|
| NFHS Statisticians' Manual .............................................................................................$8.25 |
| Scorebooks: Baseball-Softball, Basketball, Swimming & Diving, Cross Country, Soccer, | |
| Track & Field, Volleyball, Wrestling and Field Hockey ....................................................$13.00 |
| Diving Scoresheets (pad of 100)........................................................................................$11.00 |
| Volleyball Team Rosters & Lineup Sheets (pads of 100) ....................................................$11.00 |
| Libero Tracking Sheet (pads of 50)....................................................................................$11.00 |
| Baseball–Softball Lineup Sheets – 3-Part NCR (sets/100)..................................................$11.00 |
| Wrestling Tournament Match Cards (sets/100) ...................................................................$11.00 |
| Competitors Numbers (Track and Gymnastics – Waterproof, nontearable, black numbers and | |
| six colors of backgrounds numbers are 1-1000 sold in sets of 100 ........................$15.00/set |

## MISCELLANEOUS SPORTS ITEMS

| | |
|---|---|
| Court and Field Diagram Guide ....................$25.25 | From Chicago to Indy – The First 100 Years...$29.95 |
| NFHS Handbook (2023-24)..........................$15.00 | Rules PowerPoints.......................................$60.00 |
| Let's Make It Official .....................................$5.25 | Rules Changes Videos ................................$60.00 |

## ORDERING

Individuals ordering NFHS publications and other products and materials
are requested to order online at **www.nfhs.com**.

National Federation of State High School Associations

# 2023-24
# NFHS RULES BOOKS

Published in 17 sports by the National Federation of State High School Associations, rules books contain the official rules for high school athletic competition. These books are designed to explain all aspects of the game or contest. They are good for participants as well as coaches and contest officials.

The NFHS also publishes case books, manuals, handbooks and illustrated books in several sports to help in further explaining the rules.

## Customer Service Department

PO Box 361246, Indianapolis, IN 46236-5324

### 1-800-776-3462

or order online at **www.nfhs.com**

# ARE YOU READY TO JOIN?

## ANY GAME. ANYTIME. ANYWHERE.

### You are Covered!
- $6 million Annual General Liability Coverage
- $100,000 Game Call and Assigners' Coverage
- $15,500 Assault Protection
- COVID-19 Liability Coverage
- Free Consultation and Information Services

## EVERY GAME. EVERY SPORT. EVERY LEVEL.

### The Finest Training Resources
- Referee Magazine — 12 Monthly issues
- It's Official — 16-page members-only newsletter every month
- Access to NASO members-only app
- 20% discount on all Referee training products
- Exclusive discount at Ump-Attire.com
- Monthly NASO digital LockerRoom newsletter
- Online sport-specific quizzes

### For Officials, By Officials
Your dues also support NASO's efforts to improve working conditions for all sports through such efforts as:
- Assault and independent contractor legislation
- Taking informed stances on select issues in the media
- Recruitment and retention efforts
- Celebrating officials and officiating with national awards

### For more information or to join
### www.naso.org/bookjoin or call 800-733-6100

NATIONAL ASSOCIATION OF SPORTS OFFICIALS